SECRETS
OF
WINNING
ROULETTE

SECRETS OF WINNING ROULETTE

Marten Jensen

CARDOZA PUBLISHING

ABOUT THE PUBLISHER

Cardoza Publishing, publisher of *Gambling Research Institute* (GRI) books, is the foremost gaming and gambling publisher in the world with a library of almost 100 up-to-date and easy-to-read books and strategies. These authoritative works are written by the top experts in their fields and with more than five million books in print, represent the best-selling and most popular gaming books anywhere.

ACKNOWLEDGEMENTS
To DeAnna Bourdages, whose astute suggestions and skillful manuscript editing were invaluable.

First Edition

Library of Congress Catalogue Card No: 97-94710
ISBN: 0-940685-95-7

Write for your free catalogue of gaming and gambling books, advanced strategies and computer games.

CARDOZA PUBLISHING
P.O. Box 1500, Cooper Station, New York, NY 10276
Phone (718)743-5229 • Fax (718)743-8284
E-mail: Cardozapub@aol.com
www.cardozapub.com

TABLE OF CONTENTS

INTRODUCTION

The game of roulette has always been very popular in European casinos. Unfortunately, this is not true in the United States. During the last few years, however, roulette has undergone a number of changes that appear to be expanding its acceptance. This is especially evident in Las Vegas. These changes include the greater prevalence of single-zero roulette wheels, the use of electronic reader boards, and the raising of maximum bet limits. Consequently, roulette is becoming a more winnable game. One of the objectives of this book is to show how ordinary players can take advantage of this situation.

This book is an educational tool for anyone who wants to learn everything useful there is to know about the game of roulette. It is also a valuable resource for people who want to avoid being scammed in a dishonest game, by teaching them to recognize every effective method that has been and is being used to rig a roulette wheel. Of course, it is also for those players who would like to learn about the numerous techniques and systems that have been used by the professional gamblers who consistently prevail over the casino advantage.

The modern form of roulette has been around for two centuries and, during that period, gambling hall operators have devised many ways to rig roulette wheels to increase their profits. At the same time, ingenious gamblers have devised many techniques, strategies, and devices for overcoming the house advantage. This book presents every effective method of exploiting or manipulating the game, whether by the player or the house, whether easy or difficult, whether legal or not.

These methods can be grouped into four general categories; the first category being: *Biased Wheels.* Millions of dollars have been lost by casinos not paying attention to the fact that some of their wheels are biased. Most of them do very little to mitigate this potential profit risk, so it continues to be worth exploiting. This book explains the various causes for wheel bias and the best ways to identify those wheels that consistently favor certain numbers.

The second category is: *Betting Systems.* Many authors of gambling books have disparaged the use of the classical roulette betting systems. The only explanation for this attitude is that they haven't actually used and studied the systems in any depth. Like card counting in blackjack, proper system play is not a trivial exercise, and doing it the right way can be quite profitable. All the classical betting systems are described, along with recommendations on how to best apply them and details of the methods needed to mitigate their weaknesses.

The third category is: *Ball Control.* A roulette ball can be dishonestly controlled by any number of methods. Since the early days of roulette, the game operators have figured out ways to secretly rig their wheels so that they can control when and where the ball drops, or which number pockets the ball will favor. Ingenious players have also devised ways to control the ball from outside the wheel itself, usually by magnetic means. Player rigging, however, is almost a vanishing art because of protective measures that have been installed by the casinos. Wheel gaffing by casino operators, however, is alive and well, especially at illegal gambling houses, or casinos in places that have ineffective inspection procedures.

The last category is: *Prediction.* This is the art and science of predicting the winning number span each time the ball is spun, and making that prediction early enough to place appropriate bets before the dealer disallows further betting. If you think this is beyond the realm of possibility, you will be surprised to learn that there is more than one way to accomplish this feat. The oldest way is called *visual tracking.* This is a technique requiring considerable concentration and visual acuity, and is a skill that has been performed by many people for a long time. An entire chapter is devoted to describing how it can be done. The newest way is called *computer prediction*. This is another notable technique that has been successfully accomplished since shortly after the development of the first microprocessor chip in the late 1970's. To show that it is possible, a computer prediction system is described in sufficient detail that it could be duplicated by a competent programmer and a skilled electronic technician. Actual implementation of a computer prediction system, however, is not encouraged.

If you are serious about mastering any of these skills and techniques, you should not gloss over the first seven chapters which contain some very fundamental information. To fully understand some of the exploitation methods, it is necessary to learn at least a little about how the game should be played, its basic traits and peculiarities, its mathematics, and its hardware. Don't overlook the bibliography in the back of the book, which lists some good reference works. And whenever you run across an unfamiliar term, be sure to look it up in the glossary.

WHY ROULETTE?

Roulette is the oldest of all the casino games being played today, and the modern roulette wheel has been the dominant symbol of casino gambling for more than two hundred years. Whether it is a scene in a movie or TV show, or simply a photograph of a casino gaming room, the roulette wheel is usually visible and is frequently the center of attention. In many European casinos, roulette accounts for more than half the legal gaming revenue, and is so popular that getting a seat at a roulette table is often a challenge. Although most people in the United States are acquainted with roulette wheels, the game has never been very fashionable. Roulette accounts for less than five percent of total casino revenues in the U.S.

In Europe, there are few casinos in which roulette wheels are not the main focus of interest. The chief reason for this is the prevalence of the single-zero French roulette wheel, which has more favorable odds than the double-zero American wheel. In fact, in Europe, the only game with more favorable odds than roulette is baccarat.

Many newer casinos in the United States have been doing their best to make roulette more attractive to their patrons. They may be succeeding because the popularity of the game has clearly been on the rise. Three main changes have contributed to this recent phenomenon:

1. A definite trend of more casinos installing single-zero wheels has been observed. In fact, when the Monte Carlo Resort & Casino in Las Vegas opened in 1996, every one of its ten roulette wheels was a single-zero type, presumably in keeping with its name.

2. All the newer casinos have installed electronic reader boards at the roulette wheels. Many older casinos are also fitting their wheels with this type of display equipment. Reader boards continuously list the latest winning numbers in order of occurrence, and they appear to be attracting more people to the roulette wheels.

3. In many casinos, the maximum limit on both inside and outside bets has been dramatically increased. This was done with little or no change in the minimum bet requirement. As explained ilater on, a higher maximum limit can be advantageous for system players.

These recent changes in the American roulette scene are quite profound in that the game is becoming much more approachable for the average player. Now is definitely the time to learn the vulnerabilities of roulette as it is clearly developing into a very winnable game—especially for knowledgeable players.

This book will show many ways to overcome the house percentage, and reveal that roulette is no longer as hard to beat as most gambling experts seem to think. Although roulette has a colorful history of successful scams and cheating methods, there are some very legitimate ways of prevailing over the house edge. For those players who are willing to put in the necessary time and effort, roulette can be a profitable venture.

A Bit of History
It has been said that roulette, in one form or other, is as old as the wheel itself. In fact, its origins have been lost in history. However, most historians agree that the modern roulette wheel configuration and game rules were developed in France more than 200 years ago, where it has been popular ever since.

One of the earliest descriptions of this modern form of roulette can be found in the French novel *La Roulette ou le Jouer* by Jacques Lablee, which was published in 1801. In the novel, the wheel is described as having ball pockets with the numbers 1 through 36 plus two extra pockets marked with a zero and a double zero. The 0 and 00 pockets were reserved for the bank and represented the casino's mathematical advantage. The novel also describes the French betting layout very much as it appears today.

When the casino in Homburg, Germany opened in 1843, the first single-zero roulette wheel was introduced in a successful ploy to take business away from other European casinos. As will be explained later, the single-zero wheel is more advantageous to the player and pays off better than the double-zero wheel. Twenty years later, when the casino in Monte Carlo was rebuilt and reorganized, single-zero wheels were installed to insure the casino's popularity. Monte Carlo became so successful that it set the gaming standards for the rest of Europe. Ultimately, any European casino that expected to stay in business had little choice but to install single-zero wheels.

During the mid-nineteenth century, a few surplus double-zero French wheels found their way from Europe to New Orleans. At that time, the standard wheel in the United States had 28 numbered pockets plus three house pockets marked with a 0, a 00, and an eagle. Typically, the house paid single-number odds at only 26 to 1, giving it an enormous 12.9 percent advantage. Because of this, it was not a very popular game.

When single-number odds were paid at 35 to 1, the double-zero French wheel had a house advantage of only 5.26 percent. This was much better than the 12.9 percent edge that American gamblers had been playing against. Consequently, the new wheel was greatly favored by knowledgeable players. The French terminology on the betting layout was soon replaced with English, and, before long, the 38-pocket double-zero wheel became the standard roulette wheel in the United States.

Beating the Game
Because of the continuing demand, the fabrication of gaffed (rigged) roulette wheels has always been a thriving business. Illegal gambling halls always have, and still are, bilking unsuspecting

players with their gaffed roulette wheels. An entire chapter is devoted to descriptions of the most common ways that casinos have rigged their wheels. This information will help the observant player to recognize the characteristics of a gaffed wheel. Then, when one is identified, the player can either walk away from it or devise a strategy for taking advantage of it.

Operating on the premise that turnabout is fair play, the house edge has been nullified countless times by ingenious players using a variety of mechanical, magnetic, or sleight-of-hand techniques. As the casinos gradually learned of these methods, they introduced their own countermeasures, such as the installation of plastic security shields and the use of magnetic-field detectors.

Although, casino defenses have thwarted most of the older methods, bright and clever people are still at work devising new ways to do the job. One technique is the use of a computer to predict where the ball will land. The idea of using a computer, however, is not all that new. At least one attempt to devise a roulette prediction program occurred more than twenty-five years ago, a difficult project considering the size and weight of computers at that time. In recent years, modern technology brought us the pocket computer, which has opened new and exciting vistas.

Legitimate ways of beating the odds include the application of mathematical betting systems and the exploitation of biased wheels. Casinos claim to love systems players, because most of them end up losing their stake. The casinos, however, do not talk about those few system players that win consistently, but we will. Now that the number of single-zero wheels in the U.S. is growing and many casinos are raising their maximum bet limits, new life is being pumped into the classical betting systems.

We will also talk about methodical ways of finding biased wheels and why most of them are not shut down by the casinos. When one is found, it can be a gold mine.

At some point, we will cover the fundamentals of visual tracking.

This is an old technique for roulette prediction that takes advantage of partially-biased wheels.

The increase in roulette popularity should escalate as books, such as this one, contribute to a greater insight and understanding of the game. With the information provided, astute players should be able to prevail over the house advantage most of the time—even on a double-zero wheel.

Types of Roulette Wheels

Different kinds of roulette wheels are used in different parts of the world. To avoid any confusion at the outset, the main types of wheels are briefly defined and described below. Greater detail on the configuration and construction of the wheels will be found in later chapters. The main purpose for these descriptions is to establish the terminology used throughout this book. Whenever unfamiliar terms are encountered, the reader should refer to the glossary at the back of the book.

The American Wheel

The roulette wheel that is prevalent in the United States is generally called the *American wheel*. Its wheelhead (the rotating center piece) contains 38 numbered ball pockets that are alternately red and black, as shown in Figure 1-1. In addition to the numbers 1 through 36, there is a 0 and a 00, which is why the American wheel is often called a double-zero wheel.

The sequence of the numbers around the wheelhead will be called the American number sequence, to distinguish it from the French number sequence, which is entirely different. Other distinctions from the French wheel are that the betting layout terminology is in English and that non-value colored roulette checks are used to differentiate bets placed by the various players. For all bets and bet combinations except one, the house advantage for the American wheel is 5.26 percent. In Atlantic City only, the surrender rule is in effect, reducing the house edge to 2.63 percent for even-money outside bets. The surrender rule is essentially the same as the *le partage* rule used in the United Kingdom.

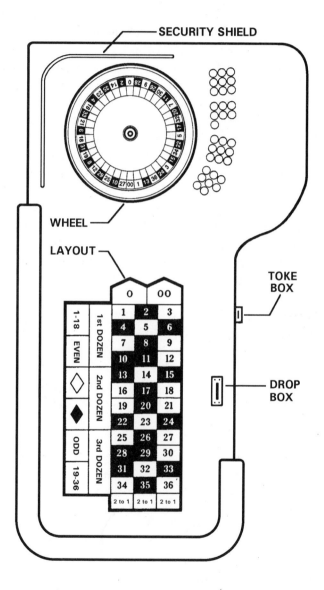

Figure 1-1 American Roulette Table

The French Wheel

The roulette wheel that is prevalent in continental Europe is called
the *French wheel*. Its wheelhead contains 37 numbered ball pockets that are alternately red and black, as shown in Figure 1-2. In
addition to the numbers from 1 through 36, there is a 0, but no
00, thus the French wheel is often called a single-zero wheel.

The sequence of numbers around the wheelhead is unique to
French wheels and will, therefore, be called the French number
sequence. As expected, the betting layout uses French terminology. Regular casino chips are used for placing bets on the layout.
Since everyone uses the same types of chips, occasionally a problem arises as to which player placed a winning chip.

The lack of a double zero is the main distinguishing factor from
the American wheel, and this reduces the house advantage for
the French wheel to 2.7 percent for all inside bets. Moreover, the
en prison rule reduces the house edge to 1.35 percent for even-
money outside bets.

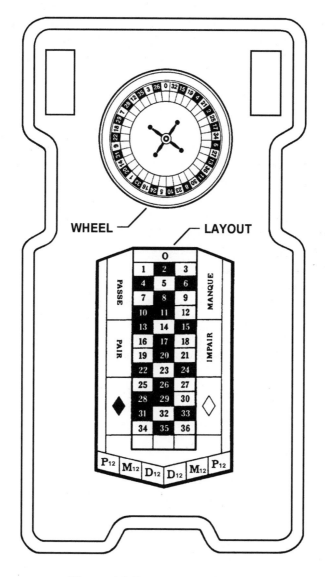

Figure 1-2 French Roulette Table

The Hybrid Wheel

A third type of wheel that is becoming more common can be described as an American-style wheel with only a single zero. Since this roulette wheel uses both French (single-zero) and American (English-language layout) characteristics, we will call it a *hybrid wheel*. This is the only kind of wheel that is legal in the United Kingdom.

The hybrid wheel, which is also used in other parts of the world, can appear with several variations. The major variation is the number sequence on the wheelhead, which may be either French or American. The position of the zero on wheels using the American number sequence is also not consistent. Sometimes the single zero is between the numbers 1 and 27, where the double-zero was originally located, and sometimes it is between the 2 and the 28. No matter what the variation, if the wheel has just a single zero and an English-language betting layout, we will call it a hybrid.

Because the hybrid wheel has 37 pockets and no double zero, the house advantage for inside bets is the same as for the French wheel: 2.70 percent. The *le partage* rule, which is used in England and is very similar to the *en prison* rule, reduces the house edge to 1.35 percent for even-money outside bets.

In those instances where a single-zero roulette wheel is used in an open casino in the United States, it is almost always a hybrid wheel. But the surrender or *le partage* rule is not applied to single-zero wheels, even in Atlantic City.

Finally, a single-zero roulette wheel with an English-language layout is often called a single-zero American wheel. To maintain consistency, this book will always call it either a hybrid wheel or a single-zero wheel, depending on the context. The term American wheel will be strictly reserved for wheels containing a double zero.

Boule and Vingt-Trois

These are roulette-like games that are mainly popular in France, Switzerland, Macau, and Malaysia. In both games, a rubber ball is spun around in a wooden bowl, eventually coming to rest in a numbered cup or cavity. There are several versions of boule, differing mainly in the number of cups (18, 25, or 36) and whether or not the bowl rotates. Vingt-trois has 27 cups and is very similar to boule.

In all countries except Switzerland, the house enjoys an 11.11 percent edge on most bets in either boule or vingt-trois, so they can only be described as sucker games. In Switzerland, the payoff odds for boule are even less favorable, resulting in an astonishing house edge of 22.22 percent. The fact that Swiss casinos attract any customers at all, says something about the desperation of Swiss gamblers. Since there is no apparent way for a player to prevail over the house advantage in either of these games, further discussion of boule and vingt-trois is of little value.

Where are the Wheels

The American double-zero wheel is prevalent in the United States and Canada. It is also commonly found in the Bahamas and the Caribbean Islands, and in parts of Asia. Although the French and hybrid wheels still prevail in Europe, the American double-zero wheel is slowly making inroads. Fortunately, the British gaming laws have kept double-zero wheels out of the United Kingdom.

By now, we should be aware of the advantage of playing a single-zero wheel, but where are they? Although there are some in the United States and Canada, they are not always easy to find. The Appendix gives a general rundown of what types of wheels are used in the major gaming areas around the world. In addition, it lists the specific casinos in the United States and Canada that, at the time this book was published, are known to have single-zero wheels on the premises.

In addition to systems players, single-zero wheels are primarily important to those players that don't use any special methods or skills to overcome the house edge. Although most of the playing techniques described in this book are dependent on certain roulette wheel characteristics, whether or not a wheel has a double zero is usually not one of them.

PLAYING THE GAME

Compared to other table games such as craps and blackjack, playing roulette is a quiet and relaxing experience. Although it may not seem so at first glance, it is a very simple game to play and there is plenty of time between spins of the ball to consider what bets to place. You just put one or more chips on a number, the ball is spun by the dealer, and if the ball lands in a pocket with your number on it, you get paid. There are a variety of other bets that can be made, such as betting on adjacent numbers or on all the odd numbers or on all the red numbers. With one exception, the house percentage on every bet is the same, which eliminates the concern that some bets may be a better deal than others.

Before you start playing, you should buy one or more stacks of special colored chips from the dealer. Each player at the table uses chips of a different color to avoid confusion as to who placed what bet. The value of each chip will be the table minimum (usually twenty-five cents to one dollar) unless you ask the dealer to set a higher value. More on this later.

The roulette table consists of a betting layout with the wheel situated at one end of the table as shown in Figure 2-1. More often in Europe, but sometimes in the United States, a double-ended layout is used with the roulette wheel located in the center. One dealer (called a *croupier* in France) operates each layout. When the crowd gets very heavy, a second dealer, called a *checkracker* or *mucker*, helps by stacking the roulette chips.

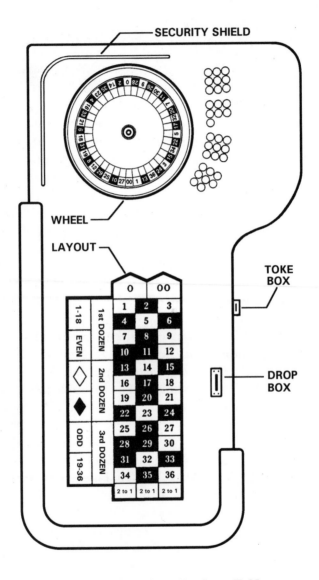

Figure 2-1 American Roulette Table

A roulette wheel consists of two major parts. The outer section is called the *bowl* and contains the circular track on which the ball spins. The rotating inner section is called the *wheelhead* and contains the numbered pockets where the ball lands and comes to rest. In an American wheel, the wheelhead has 38 separate pockets numbered from 1 to 36 (not consecutively), plus 0 and 00. The pockets are alternately colored red and black except the 0 and 00 pockets, which are colored green.

In the United States, the ball is usually spun in a clockwise direction while the wheelhead is rotating counterclockwise. In many European casinos, where the game moves at a more leisurely pace, the rotating wheelhead is stopped while the winning bets are being paid off, and then is started in the opposite direction for the next spin of the ball. In all cases, the ball is spun in the direction opposite to the wheelhead rotation.

As the game begins, the players select their bets by placing chips on the betting layout. When the dealer has finished stacking the chips accumulated from the previous game, she picks the ball out of the wheelhead and gives it a spin. The placing of bets may continue while the ball is spinning. When the ball slows down to where it has about two or three revolutions to go, the dealer calls out, "No more bets," sometimes with an accompanying pass of the hand over the layout. Any bets placed after that announcement may be disallowed by the dealer. Whether or not the dealer verbally cuts off the betting, bets placed after the ball lands in a numbered pocket are always disallowed. The placing of bets after the ball drops is called *past posting* and doing this more than once will surely attract the attention of a floor supervisor.

After the ball settles into one of the pockets, the dealer places a *win marker* on the layout at the winning number, sweeps off the losing chips and begins to pay the winners. When the payoff is complete, the dealer removes the marker and the players start placing their bets for the next spin of the ball.

Note: Whenever you encounter new terminology that is not clear from the context, please refer to the glossary at the back of this book.

Getting Started

Playing roulette is simplicity itself. First find yourself a comfortable seat at the roulette table. To reach all parts of the betting layout, the best seats are at the center of the front of the table and the last seat around the back side, next to the dealer. If the table is crowded, the first seat that opens up will have to do.

Once seated, you may buy one or more stacks of twenty colored roulette chips from the dealer. Since all the players at the table intermingle their bets on the same betting layout, each person is issued roulette chips of a different color to avoid mixups. The value of each roulette chip depends on what you paid for the stack. In Nevada, the minimum price for a 20-chip stack will be between five dollars (twenty-five cents per chip) and twenty dollars (one dollar per chip), depending on the casino and the time of day. If you pay more than the minimum, the dealer will place a special marker, called a *lammer*, on the rim of the wheel to remind her of what your particular chips are worth.

Roulette chips may be bought with cash or with regular casino chips that were obtained from the main cashier or from another table game. When you are finished playing, the dealer will exchange your remaining roulette chips back to regular casino chips. You are not allowed to remove the colored roulette chips from the roulette table—they cannot be used anywhere else and only the dealer you bought them from knows what they are worth.

Occasionally, a person will step up to the table and play cash or regular casino chips. This is usually acceptable unless a second person does the same thing, in which case the dealer might ask one of them to buy the colored roulette chips to avoid confusion.

Sooner or later you will hear the term *check*, so this is probably a good time for an explanation. The term *check* is used by casino personnel, high rollers, and professional gamblers. The term *chip* is used by everyone else. The two terms are exactly synonymous, except that if you use the term *check*, you may be perceived as an "insider." Since this book does not have any pretensions and is directed to non-insiders, it will always use the term *chip*.

Placing Bets

Bets may be made by placing one or more chips on individual numbers, on combinations of numbers, or on one of the bet areas around the outside of the number field. If a particular bet consists of more than one chip, the chips should be arranged in a single stack. If someone has already placed chips on a number you wish to bet, it is okay to stack your chips directly on top of the others. Bets for the next spin should not be placed until the dealer removes the win marker from the layout. If you forget this rule, the dealer will remind you.

Betting may continue after the dealer spins the ball, but bets should not be placed after the dealer announces, "No more bets." Bets should never be placed after the ball falls into the wheelhead, whether or not the dealer made the announcement. If you forget this rule, your bet will be disallowed. If you think that the floor supervisor is an attractive person, forgetting this rule more than once would be a way of getting acquainted.

When placing your bet, you also have to meet the minimum bet requirement for that table. In Nevada, the minimum bet usually ranges from one to five dollars; in Atlantic City, the minimum bet is five or ten dollars. If, for example, the minimum is five dollars and your chips are worth one dollar apiece, you have to bet at least five of them.

Inside Bets

There are two main categories of bets: inside bets and outside bets. All bets on the field of numbers in the center portion of the layout are called **inside bets**. These are either single-number (straight-up) bets, where the chips are placed on an individual number, or combination bets, where the chips are placed on a line between the numbers. In a combination bet, a single chip or a stack of chips can cover two through six numbers. These bets are described below.

Straight-Up Bet (One Number): A bet on a single number is called a **straight-up bet**. To place this bet properly, put the chip, or stack of chips, directly on the desired number without touching any of the borders around the number. If the bet wins, the payoff is 35 to 1. That is, for every chip that was bet on the winning number, the dealer pays out 35 chips, and you get to keep your original bet. This bet can be placed on any of the 36 numbers in the field, as well as the 0 and 00.

Split Bet (Two Numbers): A combination bet that is placed on the line between any two adjacent numbers is called a **split bet**. Position B in Figure 2-2 shows the correct place for a split bet on numbers 8 and 11. If either of the two numbers wins, the payoff is 17 to 1. That is, for every chip that was placed on the line, the dealer pays out 17 additional chips. In this bet, you are effectively splitting the value of the chip between the two numbers. If you were betting more than one chip, you could place half of the chips as a straight-up bet on each of the two adjacent numbers to get exactly the same result.

For instance, if a two-chip split bet wins, you would get 17 chips apiece for each of the two chips in your bet for a total payout of 34 chips. Since you get to keep the original bet of two chips, your profit would be 36 chips. If instead, you placed a straight-up bet on two different numbers with each of those two chips and one of the numbers won, you would get back 35 chips. Of the two chips you bet, one would have been on a losing number. But, since you get to keep the winning chip, your profit would also be 36 chips. This logic applies to all the other inside combination bets as well.

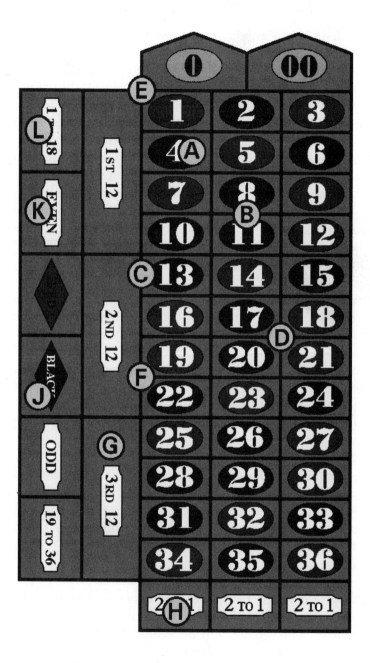

Figure 2 -2 American Betting Layout

Street Bet (Three Numbers): A **street bet** is a three-number combination bet on any of the three-number rows on the layout. To place this bet, put the chip, or stack of chips, on the outside border next to the first number in the row. Position C in Figure 2-2 shows the correct place for a street bet on numbers 13-14-15. If one of the three numbers wins, the payoff is 11 to 1.

Corner Bet (Four Numbers): A **corner bet** is a four-number combination bet on any square block of four numbers. This is also called a **square bet**. To place this bet, put the chip, or stack of chips, on the intersection of the horizontal and vertical lines in the center of a block of four numbers. Position D in Figure 2-2 shows the correct place for a corner bet on numbers 17-18-20-21. If one of the four numbers wins, the payoff is 8 to 1.

Sucker Bet (Five Numbers): There is only one **five-number bet** on the layout, and it is made by placing the chip on the left line intersection between the 1 and the 0, as shown by position E in Figure 2-2. This bet covers the numbers 0-00-1-2-3. It is called a sucker bet because the payoff is only 6 to 1. To be mathematically equivalent to the other roulette bets, the payoff should really be 6.2 to 1. As a result, the house advantage for this bet is 7.90 instead of 5.26 percent. Because there is no 00, the five-number bet does not exist on French or hybrid roulette wheels.

Line Bet (Six Numbers): A **line bet** is a six-number combination bet on two adjacent rows, thus, it is also called a **double street bet**. Chips are placed like a street bet except that they are placed at the intersection between two rows. Position F in Figure 2-2 shows the correct place for a line bet on numbers 19-20-21-22-23-24. If one of the six numbers wins, the payoff is 5 to 1.

Although the line bet covers six sequential numbers on the betting layout, these numbers do not appear sequentially on the wheelhead. The relationship between the numbers on the betting layout and the numbers on the wheelhead will be covered later.

Outside Bets

All bets outside of the main field of numbers are called **outside bets**. There are a variety of bets that include the columns, the dozens, black, red, odd, even, low (1-18) and high (19-36). Each of these bets is described below.

Dozens: The betting layout is divided into three groups of twelve numbers each, which are called the **dozens**. They are usually designated as "**1st 12**" (numbers 1 through 12), "**2nd 12**" (numbers 13 through 24), and "**3rd 12**" (numbers 25 through 36). Sometimes they are called "**1st DOZEN**", "**2nd DOZEN**", and "**3rd DOZEN**." Note that the 0 and 00 are not included in any of the three groups of dozens, so that if the winning number is 0 or 00, all dozens bets lose. Position G in Figure 2-2 shows the correct place for a dozens bet on numbers 25 through 36. If one of the twelve numbers in your group wins, the payoff is 2 to 1.

Columns: The betting layout is divided into three columns of twelve numbers each. At the bottom of each column of numbers is a box marked "2 to 1", which is the place to make a **column bet**. Note that the 0 and 00 are not a part of any column, so that if the winning number is 0 or 00, all column bets lose. Position H in Figure 2-2 is an example of a column bet. As the notation in the box indicates, the payoff is 2 to 1, same as for the dozens.

Color: At the center of the outside betting area, below the "2nd 12" box, are two diamonds, one is red and the other is black. Sometimes the words "**RED**" and "**BLACK**" appear in these boxes. This is where you can bet on either the eighteen red or the eighteen black numbers. Note that the 0 and 00 are neither black nor red—they are green. These numbers represent the house edge. If the winning number is 0 or 00, all color bets lose. Position J in Figure 2-2 shows the correct place for a bet on the black numbers. The payoff for a winner is even money (1 to 1).

Even or Odd: On either side of the color diamonds are boxes marked "**EVEN**" and "**ODD**". These are areas where a bet can be placed on the eighteen even or eighteen odd numbers. Although, in mathematics, zero is considered to be an even number, this is not true in roulette. The numbers 0 and 00 are losers for anyone who has bet on even or odd. Position K in Figure 2-2 shows the correct place for a bet on the even numbers. The payoff for a winner is even money (1 to 1). That is, for every chip in the winning stack, the dealer pays out 1 additional chip.

Low or High: At the corners of the outside betting layout, are boxes marked "**1-18**" and "**19-36**", which is where you can place a bet on the eighteen low numbers (1 through 18) or the eighteen high numbers (19 through 36). Note that 0 and 00 are not included in the low or high number groups, so that these numbers are losers for anyone that has bet either low or high. Position L in Figure 2-2 shows the correct place for a bet on the low numbers. The payoff for a winner is even money (1 to 1).

The Payoffs

Now comes the best part. If you placed a single-number (straight-up) bet on the number that won, the dealer will place the win marker on your chips and pay you 35 to 1 odds. That is, you get to keep your original bet and are paid 35 additional chips for every chip you had on the winning number. If you only placed an outside bet such as odd or even or black or red, the payoff is merely even money. If you prefer a happy medium, you can bet on the various combinations.

The following list shows all of the bet payoff odds for roulette. The letters are keyed to Figure 2-2.

A. Single numbers (straight-up)	Pays 35 to 1
B. Two numbers (split)	Pays 17 to 1
C. Three numbers (street)	Pays 11 to 1
D. Four numbers (corner)	Pays 8 to 1
E. Five numbers	Pays 6 to 1
F. Six numbers (line)	Pays 5 to 1
G. Dozen (12 numbers)	Pays 2 to 1
H. Column (12 numbers)	Pays 2 to 1
I. Red or black (18 numbers)	Pays even
J. Odd or even (18 numbers)	Pays even
K. High or low (18 numbers)	Pays even

Many casinos have information cards stacked next to the wheel showing the roulette layout and listing the bet payoffs (so you do not have to cut up this book). The above list was taken from one of those little cards.

Experienced dealers in the major casinos rarely make payoff errors, but in some smaller places it would be prudent to watch carefully. Except for the five-number bet, all bets have the same house advantage. The five-number bet, which consists of the numbers 0, 00, 1, 2, and 3, only exists on the American wheel. It gives the house a 7.90 percent advantage and, under normal circumstances, is never recommended.

Neighbors

The term *neighbors* refers to adjacent numbers on the wheelhead. In most casinos outside the United States, a player may call out a number and ask the dealer to place a neighbors bet. This would be a straight-up bet on each of three or five numbers that are next to each other on the wheelhead. The player does not need to know the wheelhead number sequence, but only has to specify the central number for the group. The dealer keeps track of the bet by using a special marker. Since each of the numbers is a straight-up bet, if any one of them wins, the payoff is 35 to 1.

Special Rules

In some casinos, a special rule gives players a second chance to win an even-money outside bet if the winning number is 0 or 00. An outside bet is defined as any of the betting options on the layout outside the main field of numbers. These bets pay either 2 to 1 or even money. The special rule applies only to those outside bets that pay even money, namely, Red, Black, Even, Odd, Low (1-18), and High (19-36). The three variations of this rule are explained below.

En Prison

This rule is applied only to the French wheel and is in effect at most European casinos and other casinos using French wheels. Whenever the winning number is 0, a player who has placed an even-money outside bet has the option of losing half the bet or allowing the entire bet to be held over (imprisoned) for the next spin. This reduces the house advantage on a French wheel from 2.70 to 1.35 percent for even-money outside bets.

Le Partage

This rule, which is applied throughout the United Kingdom, is similar to the *en prison* rule, except that the player loses half the bet and does not have the option of letting it ride. The monetary result is the same, in that the house advantage is reduced from 2.70 to 1.35 percent for even-money outside bets.

Surrender

This rule is applied only to the American double-zero wheel and is in effect in Atlantic City. It is identical to the *le partage* rule except that it is applied when the winning number is either 0 or 00. The rule reduces the house advantage on an American wheel from 5.26 to 2.63 percent for even-money outside bets.

Advice For New Players

1. When you first sit down at a roulette table, the best time to buy in is right after the dealer has finished making payoffs and has removed the win marker from the layout. The same applies to

buying additional stacks. You may buy in with cash or with regular casino chips.

2. Do not place any new bets until the dealer has removed the win marker from the layout.

3. Place your bets with reasonable care. If you win a straight-up bet, but your chip was (unintentionally) touching one of the lines around the number, it may be interpreted as a split bet, which pays only 17 to 1.

4. If another bettor has already placed chips on the number you want to bet, just put your chips directly on top of the others. If the number wins, the dealer will sort out the different colored chips and make the appropriate payoffs. If the number loses, it doesn't matter because the chips will just get swept off the layout.

5. Do not place any bets after the ball has dropped into the wheelhead. (This rule, of course, does not apply if you are a professional past poster.)

6. Do not walk off with any colored roulette chips; the chips stay with the table. If, for example, you have to go to the rest room, you have no choice but to cash in your chips and give up your seat. It's just as well; you have probably been at that table too long, anyway.

As you can see, roulette is a relaxed and leisurely diversion. There is no pressure on the player to make fast betting decisions, and the bankroll requirements (for ordinary play) is less than for most other casino table games. In later chapters, you will learn about techniques that can make this game quite profitable.

THE QUIRKS OF ROULETTE

Roulette probably has more casino-originated quirks and eccentricities than any other table game. As part of the groundwork for learning successful playing techniques, understanding the impact that these sundry peculiarities have on the game is important. The more paranoid pit bosses and floor supervisors use little ploys that they believe will impede anyone trying to predict where the ball might land, or that will break a streak of luck. Being aware of these gimmicks is helpful in determining whether or not they have a significant effect on the particular playing technique being applied.

Biased Roulette Wheels

Although a roulette wheel is supposed to be a random device, the idea of a perfectly-random roulette wheel is a myth. The high-quality wheels used in most casinos are made to tight tolerances and are precisely balanced. However, small irregularities in the construction of new wheels are unavoidable and may spawn non-random traits after a few years of heavy use. If these non-random traits become sufficiently pronounced, they can be of great advantage to the player.

Because of the counter-rotation of the ball and the wheelhead, many people think that randomness is guaranteed. Not so. Almost all roulette wheels are biased. The problem for the player is to find those wheels with a strong enough bias to overcome the house edge. Although most biases occur accidentally, a wheel can be deliberately set up to favor particular numbers or colors.

It is fortunate for the biased-wheel player, that most of the little gimmicks and ploys used by casinos to break a streak of luck are not effective against a truly-biased wheel. The only way a casino can counteract a biased wheel is either to fix it or take it out of service. In actual fact, if a wheel continues to generate good revenue, the casino is not likely to remove it from the floor.

Ball Bounce

Like piano keys, roulette balls at one time were made of ivory. Today most of them are molded out of materials such as acetal, nylon, or phenolic. Although the material a ball is made out of is not easy to determine without close examination, it is an important factor because it directly affects its liveliness. A lively, bouncing ball makes number prediction more difficult and is generally avoided by visual trackers or anyone using an advance prediction scheme. On a biased wheel, however, a lively ball is desirable because it will cross more pockets before it finally stays put. This gives it a better chance of getting trapped in the biased section of the wheel.

Many casinos use lively balls to discourage number prediction, however, there are disadvantages. If a ball gets too lively, it may bounce clear out of the wheelhead onto the table or floor. This is not only a little embarrassing, but it slows the game and reduces the take. The other disadvantage to the casino is that when a lively ball bounces across many pockets before it settles down, it has a greater chance of being caught by a loose or high fret. Thus, a lively ball can intensify a bias that otherwise might not have been playable.

Wheelhead Speed

In the larger and more elite casinos, where the roulette wheels are carefully maintained, the dealer usually keeps the wheelhead turning at a moderately slow speed—typically three to four seconds per revolution. This is how it should be. The winning number is always easy to see and there is practically no chance that the ball will ever be kicked out of the wheelhead.

In smaller casinos, however, the wheels may not be maintained as well and sometimes slow down quickly due to worn or dry bearings. To compensate for this, the dealer will often keep the wheelhead rotating faster. Furthermore, pit bosses in the smaller casinos are less experienced and more paranoid, and a faster-turning wheelhead raises their comfort level. They think if the wheelhead rotates faster, it will be harder to beat. Occasionally, the wheelhead is rotating so fast that, when the ball lands in a pocket, the dealer has to slow it down to determine the winning number. Astute players avoid such situations.

Some floor supervisors have heard that players using visual prediction methods need to have the wheelhead rotating at a particular speed to be accurate, but they do not know what speed that is. To cover themselves, they instruct the dealer to vary the speed on a regular basis. This is annoying to the visual tracker, but has little effect on a computerized prediction system. In fact, while a person is in the process of characterizing a wheel with a pocket computer, it allows the computer to store a wider range of wheelhead velocities.

Ball Switching

In many casinos, the dealer has two or three spare balls at the roulette table so that she can switch balls at will. Ball switching is often done when a player is winning consistently. It is akin to changing dice at a craps table or opening a new deck of cards at a blackjack table. Most of the time the dealer does not know what physical effect it has, but it is a standard casino ploy used to break a player's lucky streak.

The extra balls at a roulette table are frequently of varying diameters, typically 3/4-, 13/16-, and 7/8-inch. The accuracy of a prediction program that was set up for one size of ball may be adversely affected when a different size ball is substituted, especially a switch from the largest to the smallest or vice-versa.

Ball switching probably started years ago when casino operators discovered that some players were using external electromagnets to control the ball drop. For the electromagnet to work, a ball with an iron or steel slug in the center had to be substituted for the regular casino ball, a cute trick that was usually done by an accomplished sleight-of-hand artist. At that time, having the dealer occasionally switch balls was a fairly effective defense against this scam. Today, the smarter casinos check their roulette balls regularly with a magnetic stud finder or small compass.

Dealer's Signature

Every dealer puts a different spin on the ball when she launches it. The force of the initial launch, the amount and direction of english (lateral spin), or lack of english, is collectively known as the dealer's signature. Added to that should be consistency. Unless the dealer launches the ball in a consistent manner, spin after spin, the signature would be too variable for the other characteristics to have any meaning.

When a new dealer takes over a table, the dealer's signature changes. Floor supervisors believe that changing the dealer's signature by rotating dealers can effectively thwart a player that may be beating the game using unsavory means. This is another one of those ploys that falls in the category of 'it might not help, but it won't hurt.'

In any attempt to beat a roulette wheel, playing against a consistent dealer is always easier, but the actual dealer's signature makes little, if any, difference. Experiments performed with a movie camera have shown that the initial english on a roulette ball dissipates within about the first four or five revolutions around the ball track. The ball then settles down and rolls naturally with little or no lateral spin.

When a ball is launched, it typically circles the track for at least 20 revolutions before it drops. In all methods of prediction, whether visual or with a computer, the ball is not timed more than five or six revolutions ahead of the drop-off point. By that time, the dealer's initial launch speed and english would appear to have little or no effect.

Ball Speed

American casinos have learned that many roulette players like to place their bets while the ball is spinning around the track. For some compulsive players there seems to be an urgency to place bets just before the ball drops or the dealer cuts off the betting. As long as there is plenty of betting activity at the table, most casinos like their dealers to do long spins—at least 20 or 25 revolutions—to give the players more time to lay down their bets. This is a good situation for the visual tracker as well as for computer prediction.

When only two or three players are at the table and there is not much betting activity, the dealers are taught to do short spins in order to speed up the game. A short spin can be as little as 4 or 5 revolutions, which is not enough to dissipate the dealer's signature. This is bad news for computer prediction and is at least an annoyance to visual trackers.

If the dealer does a short spin at a busy table with a slowly-turning wheelhead, she is probably trying to aim the ball. See below.

Ball Aiming

Sometimes a dealer will attempt to aim the ball at, or away from, a particular number. It is often a humorous situation because the dealer rarely seems to succeed. According to an acquaintance of mine who has worked the pits in Las Vegas and was a roulette dealer for many years, aiming the ball accurately is impossible to do. Although, I have also heard the opposite opinion from reputable sources, I believe these sources did not realize they were probably observing a gaffed wheel.

If you suspect a dealer is aiming the ball, there are three clues to look for. First, the ball will be launched with less force so that it travels fewer than ten revolutions before it drops. Second, the wheelhead is kept rotating at a very slow, steady speed.

The third clue is that the dealer must be watching the wheelhead for a few moments until the numbers rotate to a predetermined position. Because they are easier to recognize than the other numbers, the dealer usually selects the green 0 or 00 as her reference and waits until the chosen number is passing under her hand before she launches the ball. You can spot this by observing the dealer's eyes when she releases the ball.

If you see only two out of the three clues, the dealer may be trying to aim the ball, but has no chance of being successful. If the dealer is not watching the wheelhead at the time the ball is launched, you can be certain it is not being aimed.

Ball Aiming Futility

One lazy weekday afternoon, while experimenting with a pocket computer at the Riverside Casino in Laughlin, I witnessed two dealers trying very hard to aim the ball. A distinguished-looking Oriental gentleman had been quite lucky playing dollar chips on the same group of numbers over and over. Each time he won a stack, he gave about a third of the stack to the dealer as a tip. Looking for more big tips, the dealer tried her very best to place the ball in one of his numbers. She had slowed the wheelhead to where it was barely rotating at all and launched the ball with so little force that it only took three or four turns to drop. She was not very successful.

Although the floor supervisor was aware of the situation, he did not try to stop it. (He was probably getting a cut of the toke pool.) This was a good example of a typical casino attitude: If the casino is not losing money and nobody is unhappy, anything goes.

The Riverside Casino has only one roulette wheel, which is in the center of a table with a double-ended betting layout. After a while, the dealer at the other side of the table began noticing the unusual actions, and before long, the two dealers were whispering to each other and doing a lot of giggling. My partner and I seemed to be the only persons that noticed these antics, probably because it was screwing up my computer program.

When the shift rotated, the other dealer moved to our side of the table and tried the same thing. Nothing worked and the gentleman eventually lost all his chips and left. This silliness went on for almost an hour, during which time my computer was totally ineffective. Of course, we had no choice but to grin and bear it, but it was a fascinating demonstration of ball-aiming futility.

Foreign Casinos

To a person that has mastered the game and developed winning playing techniques, the idea of playing roulette in foreign casinos can be fascinating. The table limits are higher, the payoff odds are better and, compared to Las Vegas or Atlantic City, it can be quite an exotic experience.

Since most foreign casinos use single-zero wheels, the house advantage is only 2.70 percent, and can be as low as 1.35 percent for even-money outside bets. Furthermore, in the classier European casinos, the permissible maximum bet is usually much higher than in most U.S. casinos.

If you are going abroad and intend to visit any casinos, obtain information ahead of time about the local gambling rules. If you wait until arriving at your destination, you may be disappointed because of a lack of advanced preparation. For example, some casinos have a strict dress code and require semi-formal evening wear.

In the United Kingdom, because all casinos are private clubs, admission is restricted to members and their guests. If you don't know a club member, you will have to submit a membership application form after you arrive and wait at least 24 hours before you will be allowed admission.

Before you go to a lot of trouble disguising your electronic equipment to get it past X-ray machines and foreign customs (they get very nosey about anything that looks electronic), there are a few things you should know. Although the French wheel gives the player better odds, it has a different type of ball track that makes it more difficult to predict where the ball will drop, especially with the computer method. Instead of an abrupt drop-off, the ball spirals down from the track until it strikes one of the deflectors, after which, its motion is totally unpredictable.

Even in casinos where American-style wheels are used, other problems can be encountered. For instance, in the Orient, the standard routine is to cut off betting before the dealer launches the ball. This eliminates visual tracking and any method that is dependent on ball timing. However, it does not curtail the exploitation of a biased wheel.

In Latin America you have to be flexible, because in many countries the gambling situation is unstable and major changes can occur with little warning. If you manage to come out ahead, your winnings will be in the local currency and, often, will not be easy to get out of the country—so plan to spend the money during your stay.

In planning a trip abroad, forget the sophisticated electronics and, instead, bring a small notebook so you can spend your time looking for biased wheels. Or, if you have studied our advice , do what many Europeans do: play a system.

NUMBER GAMES

This chapter and the next cover several numerical concepts that are important to understand before engaging in any esoteric roulette wheel activities. If you are thinking of skipping this material, at least scan it so that you know what is included here when coming back to it for reference.

The Definition of Probability

Before we can grasp most mathematical ideas in the realm of gambling, we need to get a sound understanding of the meaning of probability and odds. Let us start with the following formal definition of probability and take it from there:

The probability of the occurrence of an event is defined as the number of cases favorable to the event, divided by the number of equally-likely possible cases.

If we assume that all possible outcomes are equally likely because they are generated by a random device (such as a roulette wheel), and that for each outcome there are only two possible results (win or lose), another way of defining probability would be:

The probability of winning is equal to the number of ways to win, divided by the number of possible outcomes.

Since only two results are possible (win or lose), the total number of outcomes is equal to the sum of the possible ways to win plus the possible ways to lose. This can be expressed as the following simple formula:

$$\text{PROBABILITY OF WINNING} = \frac{\text{WAYS TO WIN}}{\text{WAYS TO WIN} + \text{WAYS TO LOSE}}$$

Probability is always a number between 0 and 1 that can be stated as a fraction or a decimal. Sometimes the decimal is multiplied by 100 and expressed as a percentage. An elementary example would be the flip of a coin, which has one way to win and one way to lose. The probability of winning would then be:

$$\text{Pw A COIN FLIP} = \frac{1}{1+1} = \frac{1}{2} = 0.5$$

where Pw = probability of winning.

A statistician would say that the probability of winning the flip of a well-balanced coin is one half, or point five. A gambler would say it is 1 chance out of 2. Most other people would rather convert the 0.5 to a percentage and say that they have a fifty percent chance of winning a coin flip. In this book, we will call this a probability of 1/2.

For another example, take a standard six-sided die and determine the probability of rolling a particular number. Since there is one way to win and five ways to lose, the probability of winning would be:

$$\text{Pw A SINGLE DIE THROW} = \frac{1}{1+5} = \frac{1}{6} = 0.1667$$

The statistician would now say that the probability of correctly guessing the number is one sixth, or .1667. The gambler would say one chance out of six, while the rest of us would say it is almost seventeen percent. In this book, we will use the terminology 1/6.

On an American roulette wheel with 38 numbers, if a straight-up bet is placed on a single number, the number of ways to win is 1 and the number of ways to lose is 37. Applying the same probability formula:

$$Pw \ A \ STRAIGHT\text{-}UP \ BET = \frac{1}{1 + 37} = \frac{1}{38} = 0.0263$$

For a street bet on a row of three numbers, the number of ways to win is 3 and the number of ways to lose is 35. The probability of winning is then:

$$Pw \ A \ STREET \ BET = \frac{3}{3 + 35} = \frac{3}{38} = 0.0789$$

For a dozens bet, the number of ways to win is 12 and the number of ways to lose is 26. The probability of winning is:

$$Pw \ A \ DOZENS \ BET = \frac{12}{12 + 26} = \frac{12}{38} = 0.3158$$

By now, you should be able to figure the probability of any other bet on the roulette table.

The Meaning of Odds

Most gamblers prefer using the term *odds* instead of probability. Although they appear to be similar, there is a mathematical difference between the two terms, which is important to know. If you have calculated the probability of winning and want to know the odds for winning, use the following relationship:

$$ODDS \ FOR \ WINNING = \frac{Pw}{1 - Pw}, \ \text{where } Pw = \text{probability of winning.}$$

Using the coin-flip example from above,

$$\text{ODDS FOR WINNING} = \frac{0.5}{1 - 0.5} = \frac{0.5}{0.5} = \frac{1}{1}$$

Odds are not converted to a decimal, but are expressed as a ratio of whole numbers; thus, we had to multiply the numerator and denominator by 2 to get the desired result. The above odds are usually given as 1:1 and spoken as "one-to-one" (which is also called *even odds*).

A simpler way of doing all this is to skip the probability step and calculate the odds more directly by using the following formula:

$$\text{ODDS FOR WINNING} = \frac{\text{WAYS TO WIN}}{\text{WAYS TO LOSE}}$$

Compare this with the probability formula, above. If we try the coin-flip example, you can see that it comes out to 1:1 with no fuss at all. Now, if we try the single die example, the result is:

$$\text{ODDS FOR WINNING} = \frac{1}{5}$$

This says that the odds for winning are 1:5, which means that there is one chance to win and five chances to lose. This is different from the probability of winning, which is 1 chance out of 6—do not get them mixed up.

Another place people get confused is when the odds are stated in reverse. For instance, if the odds *for* winning are 1:5, then the odds *against* winning are 5:1, and the odds formula is inverted:

$$\text{ODDS AGAINST WINNING} = \frac{\text{WAYS TO LOSE}}{\text{WAYS TO WIN}}$$

In the above example, the distinction between *odds for* and *odds against* is obvious, but when the odds are close to even, it can be more subtle. For instance, when the odds for winning are 4:5, then the odds against winning are 5:4. While the seasoned gambler has no problem with this, the newcomer can be easily misled by interchanging the words *for* and *against*. Although not as technically correct, some people think it is clearer to say "winning odds" instead of odds for winning and "losing odds" instead of odds against winning. They have a point.

House odds or *odds paid* are the inverse of winning odds, that is, the lower the chances of winning, the higher the payoff. In the example of a single die, we saw that the odds for winning are 1:5 and the odds against winning are 5:1. Since the house is betting against the player, the odds paid are the same as the odds against winning, assuming the house does not take a cut. On an even playing field, if a 1-unit bet wins, the profit should be 5 units. In actuality, the house odds will always be a little less than the odds against winning, to give the casino its profit margin.

A subtle trick is sometimes used to make house odds look better than they are by stating the odds as 5 *for* 1, instead of 5 *to* 1. If you win a payoff of 5 *to* 1, you get paid 5 units *and* get to keep your original 1-unit bet, whereas a payoff of 5 *for* 1 means you get paid 5 units, but lose your original bet. Odds of 5 for 1 is equivalent to odds of 4 to 1. Again, the professional gambler has no difficulty with this, but less experienced players can easily get confused.

Now that we have done some groundwork on the meaning of *odds*, let us apply these facts to the roulette wheel. On an American wheel with 38 numbers, if a straight-up bet is placed on a single number, the number of ways to win is 1, and the number of ways to lose is 37. Applying the odds formula:

$$\text{ODDS FOR WINNING} = \frac{\text{WAYS TO WIN}}{\text{WAYS TO LOSE}} = \frac{1}{37}$$

Thus, the odds for winning are 1 to 37, or 1:37, and, conversely, the odds against winning are 37:1. Of course, if you do win the single number bet, the house will pay only 35:1, the difference being the house edge, which will be explained more thoroughly in the next chapter.

If a single combination bet is placed on four adjacent numbers, the number of ways to win is 4 and the number of ways to lose is 34. Thus...

$$\text{ODDS FOR WINNING} = \frac{\text{WAYS TO WIN}}{\text{WAYS TO LOSE}} = \frac{4}{34}$$

The odds for winning are then 4 to 34 and the odds against winning are 34:4. If you win this bet, the house will pay only 32:4 and take a 2-unit profit.

For an even-money outside bet, such as red, the number of ways to win is 18 and the number of ways to lose is 20 (18 blacks plus 2 greens). Thus...

$$\text{ODDS FOR WINNING} = \frac{\text{WAYS TO WIN}}{\text{WAYS TO LOSE}} = \frac{18}{20}$$

The odds for winning are 18 to 20 and the odds against winning are 20:18. For winning this bet, the house will pay 18:18, again taking their 2-unit profit.

The Concept of Randomness

Ideally, a roulette wheel is a random machine; that is, the winning numbers should always be random and unpredictable. Although the best of the modern wheels are carefully built to tight tolerances using precision fabrication techniques, there is no such thing as a perfectly-random roulette wheel. Before we can intelligently explore the various causes of wheel bias, we first need to know what is meant by random.

The notion of randomness, although seemingly simple, can be a difficult idea to understand. This lack of understanding often leads to misconceptions regarding the probability of the occurrence of a desired event. Adding to the confusion is the fact that a theoretically-random roulette wheel can generate number sequences that, in the short term, are seemingly non-random. We will try to clear up these apparent inconsistencies with rational explanations.

One place to start is with the following statistical definition of random:

A random system is a process of selection in which each item of a set has an equal probability of being chosen.

Applying the definition to an American roulette wheel, the items in the set are the 38 numbered pockets. If the wheel is truly random, each of those numbers should have an equal chance of winning at every spin of the ball. In other words, the probability of any given number winning should be exactly 1 chance out of 38. (See the previous discussion on probability.)

The simplicity of this definition, however, is somewhat misleading, because it appears to apply to only one event at a time. The fact is, that the definition also applies to any group of single events, which we will call a *compound event*. Take a simple compound event such as two sequential spins of a roulette wheel resulting in two winning numbers in sequence. The number of possible outcomes is 38 x 38 = 1444; therefore, the probability of any preselected sequence of two numbers occurring is exactly 1 chance out of 1444.

In other words, if any two numbers are selected, say 12 and 27, the probability of a 12 coming up at the next spin *and* a 27 coming up at the following spin is 1 chance out of 1444. This would also be true if the two selected numbers were the same, such as 17 and 17.

If you are keeping track of the winning numbers at a roulette wheel, the same number coming up twice in a row may occur more often than you would expect. How can this be, when the chance of this occurring is only 1 out of 1444? The answer is that the probability of 1 chance out of 1444 only applies to *preselected* numbers. When we are talking about *any* pair, the probability calculation changes. If it doesn't matter what the first number is, then it simply becomes the preselection for the second number, and the total probability is 1 chance out of 38 that the second number will be the same as the first. For an average wheel that is spun 100 times per hour, we would expect to see *any* pair occurring almost three times an hour.

In the final analysis, a truly-random process is always unpredictable and the outcome of each event is totally unaffected by previous results. This is the manner in which all casino operators hope their roulette wheels behave.

MORE NUMBER GAMES

Although the mathematical notions in this chapter are less theoretical and more pragmatic than the ones in the last chapter, they do require an understanding of probability and odds. If you are having some difficulty with those concepts, a review of our previous discussions on these matters is advised.

As defined earlier, the three basic types of roulette wheels are the American, the French, and the hybrid. From the standpoint of mathematical analysis, however, there are only two types. They will be called the single-zero wheel and the double-zero wheel. As we already know, the American wheel is a double-zero wheel with 38 numbers, while the French and hybrid wheels have a single zero and 37 numbers.

The House Advantage

The house advantage, which is also called the **house edge**, the **house take**, or **vigorish**, represents a casino's life blood, that is, its primary income. For each table game, the casino establishes payoff odds to give itself a profit on every bet made by the players. In some games the house advantage seems small, but no matter how small it seems, it still has the effect of grinding away a player's bankroll little by little.

Considering the variety of bets that can be placed at a roulette table, some people find it hard to believe that, with only one exception, the house advantage remains constant. This doubtfulness is especially true for people who are familiar with craps, since the house edge in craps varies from less than 1 percent to as high as 16.6 percent, depending on the bet. To gain some insight, it is always useful to understand how the house advantage is calculated.

Although the American wheel has 38 possible winning numbers, the payoff for a single winning number is only 35 to 1. Thus, for winning a 1-unit bet, the house pays back 35 units plus the original bet. Since the probability of winning is $1/38$ (1 chance out of 38), but we get back only 36 units, the difference of 2 units (38 minus 36) is the house edge. Now multiply the house edge by the probability of winning and convert the result to a percentage by multiplying by 100...

$$2 \times \frac{1}{38} = \frac{2}{38} = 0.0526315 \times 100 = 5.26315$$

...which rounds off to 5.26 percent.

A more generalized way of approaching this calculation would be to multiply the difference between the actual losing odds and the house odds by the probability of winning (Pw):

HOUSE ADVANTAGE = (ODDS AGAINST WINNING – HOUSE ODDS) x Pw

Converting to a percentage: HOUSE PERCENTAGE = HOUSE ADVANTAGE x 100

From the previous chapter we learned that...

$$\text{ODDS AGAINST WINNING} = \frac{\text{WAYS TO LOSE}}{\text{WAYS TO WIN}}$$

and we also learned that...

$$\text{PROBABILITY OF WINNING (Pw)} = \frac{\text{WAYS TO WIN}}{\text{WAYS TO WIN} + \text{WAYS TO LOSE}}$$

For a single straight-up bet, the odds against winning are 37:1 and the house odds are 35:1. Odds can be treated like a fraction so that 35:1 is the same as 35/1. The probability of winning is $1/(1+37) = 1/38$. Entering these numbers into the formula for HOUSE ADVANTAGE, we get:

$$\frac{37}{1} - \frac{35}{1} \times \frac{1}{38} = \frac{2}{1} \times \frac{1}{38} = \frac{2}{38} = 0.0526315$$

Then, HOUSE PERCENTAGE = 0.0526315 x 100 = 5.26 percent

Combination bets work out the same way. For a four-number combination bet, the odds against winning are 34:4 and the house odds are 8:1. The probability of winning is $4/4+34 = 4/38$. To enable subtraction of the fractions, the denominator of the house odds should be the same as for the losing odds. This is done by multiplying 8/1 by 4/4 and using the equivalent value of 32/4 for the house odds. Entering these numbers, we get:

$$\frac{34}{4} - \frac{32}{4} \times \frac{4}{38} = \frac{2}{4} \times \frac{4}{38} = \frac{2}{38} = 0.0526315$$

HOUSE PERCENTAGE = 0.0526315 x 100 = 5.26 percent

...and the result is the same as for the straight-up bet.

Now try it on an even-money bet. Let us say we bet one unit on red. Since there are eighteen red numbers, there are eighteen ways to win that bet. There are eighteen black numbers plus two green numbers, so there are twenty ways to lose. Knowing the house odds are 1:1, we will multiply by 18/18 to make the denominator of the fraction the same as for the losing odds. Plugging into the formula:

$$\frac{20}{18} - \frac{18}{18} \times \frac{18}{38} = \frac{2}{18} \times \frac{18}{38} = \frac{2}{38} = 0.0526315$$

HOUSE PERCENTAGE = 0.0526315 x 100 = 5.26 percent

...and, again, there is the same 5.26 percent.

The sole exception is a bet that can only be made on a double-zero wheel—the five-number bet. This is a combination bet on the numbers 1, 2, 3, 0, and 00, which pays off at 6 to 1. The probability of winning is 5 chances out of 38. If we do the same calculation as above, we will come up with a house advantage of 7.8947 percent. This is not a recommended bet.

If we try these calculations on the French or hybrid wheel, it will always come out to 2.7 percent. Remember, if we win a straight-up bet, the house will still pay out 35 units, but since the wheel has only 37 numbers, the calculation looks like this:

$$\frac{36}{1} - \frac{35}{1} \times \frac{1}{37} = \frac{1}{1} \times \frac{1}{37} = \frac{1}{37} = 0.02703$$

HOUSE PERCENTAGE = 0.02703 x 100 = 2.7 percent

On an even-money bet with the *en prison* rule or the *le partage* rule in effect, the house advantage is cut in half to 1.35 percent because whenever the 0 comes up, only half the bet is lost. This is the lowest house edge of any casino game, except baccarat, and is a major reason roulette is so popular in Europe.

When the surrender rule is used with the American wheel, the house advantage is also cut in half to 2.63 percent for even-money bets. The surrender rule is in effect in Atlantic City, but not in Nevada.

Overdue Numbers

In a quasi-random game, such as roulette, if a particular number has not won after an unexpectedly high number of spins (say, more than 70 or 80 spins), it seems logical that it is due to come up pretty soon. Most players believe this to be true because they do not fully understand that each spin of the ball is totally unaffected by previous events.

Unlike a computer or the human brain, a roulette wheel has no memory—none at all. A roulette wheel has no mechanism or means for remembering what number won at the previous spin of the ball, or at any earlier spin. This situation is identical to that of a pair of dice, which also cannot remember what numbers came up on the previous roll. As with the dice, each time the roulette ball is spun, the outcome is totally unaffected by history and is, therefore, called an *independent* event.

At every spin of the ball in a double-zero wheel, the probability of a preselected number winning is 1/38, or 1 chance in 38. Assume, for a moment, that the number 23 has won twice in a row. At the third spin of the ball, the probability of number 23 winning is still 1/38—the same probability as any other number on the wheel. If, on the other hand, the number 23 has not come up in the past 100 spins, the probability of number 23 winning at the 101st spin is still 1/38—no more, no less.

Repeating Numbers

Some confusion comes from the result of statistically combining two or more successive events. The combined probability of the number 23 winning twice in a row is the product of the individual probabilities: 1/38 x 1/38 = 1/1444. The probability of 23 coming up three times in a row is: 1/38 x 1/38 x 1/38 = 1/54872. The odds of this occurring gets smaller with each repetition.

Some people might say, "The third time 23 comes up, it has to beat heavy odds!" Not so—*the odds were beat on the first two spins!* That is, the first two spins (combined) overcame a probability of 1/1444. To win on the third spin, the number 23 still only has to beat a probability of 1/38. If it does win, the combined probability of all three spins is $1/1444 \times 1/38 = 1/54872$.

These odds will be true despite what has happened on previous spins, because the wheel has no memory of what occured before. If, for example, the number 23 won three times in a row, on the fourth spin the probability of 23 coming up is still 1/38. Still, they say, the odds of a given number winning four times in a row are astronomically small. That is correct, the probability of that happening is one chance in more than two million, as the following calculation shows:

$$1/38 \ \times \ 1/38 \ \times \ 1/38 \ \times \ 1/38 \ = \ 1/2085136$$

...or 1 chance in 2.085 million.

Even so, on any individual spin, the probability is still 1/38. To summarize, following is a little chart of the expected probabilities of repeating numbers.

PROBABILITY OF OCCURRENCE FOR:		
Repeats	Any number	A preselected Number
1	1/1	1/38
2	1/38	1/1444
3	1/1444	1/54872
4	1/54872	1/2085136

Note that any number repeating itself is not a rare event. As the above chart shows, a repeat is likely to occur every 38 spins, or about two to three times per hour.

Streaks and Runs

By the same reasoning, the probability of an even-money bet winning is 18/38, because there are eighteen ways to win out of 38 possibilities. If a black number won three times in succession, on the fourth spin of the ball, the probability of black winning is still 18/38. The probability of red winning is also 18/38. The same holds true for the odd, even, high eighteen, and low eighteen numbers. Each of those even-money bets has a probability of success of 18 chances out of 38, no matter what came up on the previous spin.

Now that we have the single-spin probability of winning firmly established, we can look at the probability of the occurrence of a winning streak. The probability of red winning twice in a row is the product of the individual probabilities:

$$18/38 \ \times \ 18/38 \ = \ 324/1444 \ = \ 1/4.46$$

...or once every 4.46 spins of the ball. Then it follows that the probability of red winning three times in a row is:

$$18/38 \ \times \ 18/38 \ \times \ 18/38 \ = \ 5832/54872 \ = \ 1/9.41$$

...or once every 9.41 spins of the ball. And so forth.

The probability of the occurrence of a *losing* streak, on the other hand, is a little different. On a double-zero wheel, the 0 and 00 both lose any outside bets. Thus, the probability of any even-money bet losing is 20/38, because there are 20 ways to lose. The probability of a given even-money bet losing twice in a row is:

$$20/38 \ \times \ 20/38 \ = \ 400/1444 \ = \ 1/3.61$$

...or once every 3.61 spins of the ball.

In summary, the following is a chart showing the expected frequency of even-money outside-bet winning and losing streaks for a *double-zero* wheel:

Winning Streak of	Occurs Every	Losing Streak Of	Occurs Every
1	2.1 spins	1	1.9 spins
2	4.5 spins	2	3.6 spins
3	9.4 spins	3	6.9 spins
4	19 spins	4	13 spins
5	41 spins	5	25 spins
6	89 spins	6	47 spins
7	187 spins	7	89 spins
8	395 spins	8	170 spins
9	833 spins	9	323 spins
10	1758 spins	10	613 spins
11	3712 spins	11	1165 spins
12	7837 spins	12	2213 spins
13	16544 spins	13	4205 spins
14	34927 spins	14	7990 spins
15	73734 spins	15	15181 spins
16	155660 spins	16	28844 spins

The following chart shows the expected frequency of even-money outside-bet winning and losing streaks for a *single-zero* wheel:

Winning Streak Of	Occurs Every	Losing Streak Of	Occurs Every
1	2.1 spins	1	1.9 spins
2	4.2 spins	2	3.8 spins
3	8.6 spins	3	7.4 spins
4	18 spins	4	14 spins
5	37 spins	5	28 spins
6	75 spins	6	55 spins
7	155 spins	7	106 spins
8	319 spins	8	207 spins
9	655 spins	9	403 spins
10	1347 spins	10	784 spins
11	2768 spins	11	1527 spins
12	5691 spins	12	2974 spins
13	11697 spins	13	5792 spins
14	24044 spins	14	11279 spins
15	49424 spins	15	21965 spins
16	101594 spins	16	42773 spins

Number Sequences

Many effective betting techniques require the placing of bets on groups of adjacent numbers around the wheelhead. The smarties who originally devised the number sequences for the French and American wheels apparently knew this and made it very difficult to bet contiguous sectors without having to scatter chips all over the betting layout. Memorizing the sequences is not an easy task.

Most roulette computer programs are number-sequence sensitive, that is, a program designed for the American sequence will not work properly with the French sequence, aside from the fact that the French sequence does not contain a double zero. Whenever playing a particular roulette wheel, it should be noted whether it is an American or French sequence. See Figure 5-1.

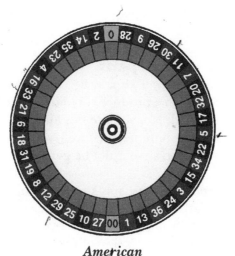

American

French

*Figure 5-1 American and French
Number Sequences*

It is also important to note that even if a wheel has just a single zero, this does not always define the number sequence. Some places in Europe and the Orient have single-zero, 37-pocket wheels with an American number sequence. See the definition of hybrid wheels earlier.

Contiguous Number Spans

The serious roulette player should be fully aware of the major betting combinations that produce contiguous number sequences around the wheelhead. No, you are not allowed to skip this section. If you do not like numbers that well, you should not be playing roulette, in fact, you should not be gambling at all.

On the American wheel, the best known contiguous bet combination is based on the center column. The center column covers the span (clockwise) from 23 to 5, with five gaps (0, 7, 9, 28 and 30) and only two numbers outside of the span. It is probably the most common bet placed by visual trackers; it covers a span width of 15 numbers, almost exactly two fifths of the wheel perimeter, as shown in Figure 5-2.

This bet can be placed in three different ways. The first is to put one chip on each of the numbers 0, 7, 9, 28 and 30, and then put a stack of four or more chips on the center column. The second way is to put one chip on the 7-8-9 row, one chip on the 28-29-30 row, and then put two or more chips on the center column. The third and fastest way is just to bet the center column and hope the ball does not fall into one of the five gaps.

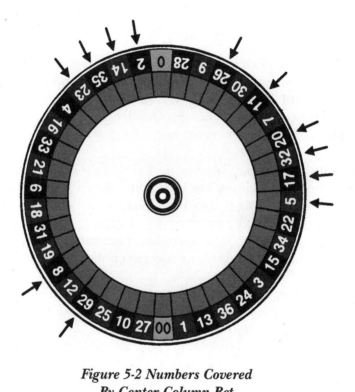

*Figure 5-2 Numbers Covered
By Center Column Bet*

There are two combinations of 3-number street (row) bets on the American wheel that are often used by professionals. These are especially good because they cover eight-number spans with no gaps. The first span goes from 22 to 1, and is fully executed by placing four street bets on 1-2-3, 13-14-15, 22-23-24 and 34-35-36. This also results in a secondary 4-number span at the opposite side of the wheel. In Figure 5-3 these spans are called Group A.

The second span covers the numbers 19 through 4, and is done by placing street bets on 4-5-6 and 31-32-33, and then placing split bets on 16-19 and 18-21. In Figure 5-3 this is called Group B. It is an especially-good combination because there are only two numbers outside of the main span.

One word of caution: Almost everyone in the business knows about the center-column bet. When pit supervisors observe some-one repeatedly using it, they may think a visual tracker is at work and will start watching carefully (although they are not sure what they are looking for). The street-bet combinations, however, are not so well known and will usually pass unnoticed.

The French wheel is a totally different story. Its number sequence is so well designed that the only easy way to lay down a contigu-ous-number bet is to request a neighbors bet. In Europe, contigu-ous-number betting is common and is tolerated by the casinos (as long as you are not a big winner). When you ask the dealer to place a neighbors bet, your bet will automatically include num-bers on both sides of your specified number.

Most single-zero wheels in the United States have the French num-ber sequence. Whether the casino operators know it or not, this makes contiguous-number betting more difficult, since most U.S. dealers do not place neighbors bets. Obviously, you should not play such a wheel when contiguous-number betting is important.

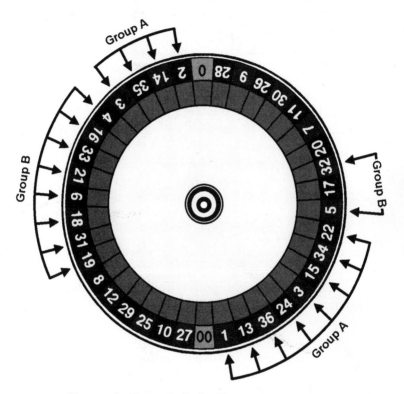

Group A: Rows 1, 5, 8, 12
Group B: Rows 2, 11; Split bets 16-19, 18-21

*Figure 5-3 Number Spans Covered
by Combination Street Bets*

ROULETTE WHEEL CONSTRUCTION

To develop more insight into the physical vulnerabilities of a roulette wheel, it is helpful to be familiar with variations in construction. Certain playing techniques are not effective with some types of wheels, so it is necessary to be able to discern the differences visually. This chapter covers the construction details and defines the terminology used for different parts of the wheel so that you understand exactly what is meant when these terms are used elsewhere in this book.

At one time, almost all the roulette wheels used in the United States were manufactured domestically by noted masters such as Benteler, Rude, Tramble, and Wills. Unfortunately, that is no longer the case. Paul Tramble of Reno was the last of the old American roulette craftsmen, and he retired in 1996. His business was bought out by Bud Jones Gaming Supplies in Las Vegas, and they are now manufacturing wheels with the Tramble name.

Today, many American casinos import their wheels from European suppliers such as John Huxley of London. These imported wheels are specially made for the U.S. market, so they have the double zero and the American number sequence. However, many of them have European-style ball tracks and low-profile ball pockets that make it more difficult for anyone trying to use a prediction technique. Consequently, learning how to distinguish between the different wheel designs is important.

In the past, the few single-zero wheels used in the United States were imported from Europe, but this is no longer true. Paulson Gaming Supplies of Las Vegas, has been making inroads with its slick-looking black plastic wheels. Paulson supplied all of the single-zero wheels at the new Monte Carlo Hotel in Las Vegas.

Basic Roulette Wheel Construction

A roulette wheel consists of two main components: the external housing, called the bowl, and the rotating center piece, called the wheelhead or cylinder. The way these structural elements correlate is shown in Figure 6-1.

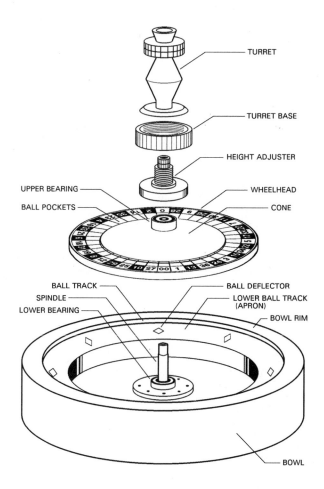

Figure 6-1 Roulette Wheel Components

In most roulette wheels, the bowl is about thirty-two inches in diameter and constructed entirely of solid wood or wood composition with wood veneer or plastic laminated surfaces. The bowl assembly contains the ball track, the lower ball track apron with the ball deflectors, and the vertical shaft or spindle that supports the wheelhead. In some wheels, the rim and ball track section of the bowl is a molded plastic subassembly.

The wheelhead, which is about twenty inches in diameter, is seated inside the bowl and rotates on a vertical spindle. It is usually fitted with upper and lower ball-bearing assemblies, but some less-expensive wheels just use a needle bearing. Along the outer edge of the wheelhead circumference is a circle of numbers and just inside the numbers are the ball pockets.

The central part of the wheelhead, inside the ring of ball pockets, is called the cone. This area slopes upward toward the center of the wheelhead and, thus, has a conical shape. The purpose of the cone is to direct a rolling ball back toward the pockets. Attached to the center of the cone is a decorative piece called a turret, which hides the height adjusting mechanism for the wheelhead.

The entire roulette wheel assembly, which is quite rigid and heavy, can be leveled by adjusting the three or four feet that are found on the bottom surface of the bowl. Most wheels also have a means for precisely adjusting the height of the wheelhead. This is important because if the outer edge of the wheelhead perimeter is too high in relation to the lower edge of the apron, a ball can get hung up there and refuse to fall into a pocket.

The Roulette Ball

At one time, all roulette balls were made of ivory because it was the only suitable material available. With the arrival of synthetics and the illegality of importing ivory, this eventually changed. Today, roulette balls are typically made from acetal, nylon, or phenolic.

If it were not for the difference in the bounce characteristic, we wouldn't care less what material was used. However, bounce is important. Almost any kind of prediction method is thwarted by a lively, bouncing ball. However, on a biased wheel, a lively ball is more desirable since it has a better chance of encountering the biased section of the wheel.

A ball that is so bouncy that it just will not settle down, is probably made from nylon. A less lively ball would likely be acetal, and a ball that falls off the track with a thud is probably molded from a phenolic material.

The New Jersey gambling laws dictate that a roulette ball has to be at least 12/16-inch and not more than 14/16-inch in diameter. A law does not appear to be needed because no matter where you go, the roulette balls will be about 13/16-inch in diameter. That is the best size to use. A smaller ball is captured sooner between the pocket frets with a minimum amount of bounce, while a larger ball settles down too fast because of its weight.

The Ball Track

From a player's viewpoint, the ball track is one of the most important components of a roulette wheel. The type of track and its condition is especially critical for a person or team using any kind of a prediction method.

Twenty years ago, the type of track was not a consideration on American wheels because they were all very similar. In recent years, however, a new track design was introduced by foreign manufacturers. Many casino operators do not realize it yet, but that new track design is probably reducing prediction success by 90 percent. An examination of Figures 6-2 and 6-3, will show the reason.

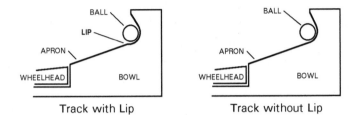

Figure 6-2 Types of Ball Tracks

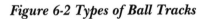

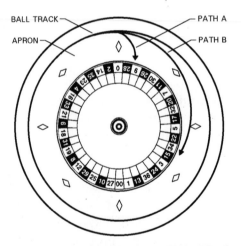

PATH A : PATH OF BALL AFTER LEAVING TRACK WITH LIP
PATH B : PATH OF BALL AFTER LEAVING TRACK WITHOUT LIP

Figure 6-3 Typical Ball Paths

The old type of ball track has a lip on which the ball rides as it circles the track. When the ball slows enough that centrifugal force can no longer hold it up, it drops off the lip of the track. If the ball then contacts one of the ball deflectors, it will bounce around before settling in a pocket. Often, however, the ball rolls between two of the deflectors straight into a pocket with very little action. Although it may bounce out again, it usually ends up within one or two pockets from the one it first entered.

This is a situation that a predictor enjoys. In wheels with the old-type track, a low-bounce ball, and deep pockets, the ball will usually (two out of three times) end up in a pocket very close to the one that was slightly ahead of the ball when it left the track. If a ten-number span is successfully predicted only half the time, the profitability can be quite good. At one unit per number, betting a ten-number spread twice would cost the predictor 20 units. If one of those spins produces a 35-unit winner, the profit would be 35 minus 19, which equals 16 units.

The main difference in the new-type track is that it has no lip. As a result, when the ball loses velocity and the centrifugal force can no longer hold it on the track, instead of falling directly into the wheelhead, it spirals around the apron at a very shallow angle. This has detrimental results for any prediction method, visual or otherwise.

Because of the shallow angle, the ball usually contacts one or more of the ball deflectors before reaching the pockets. When this happens, the motion of the ball becomes quite unpredictable, and it may end up almost anywhere on the wheelhead. Even if it slides past the deflectors, because of the spiral path, it is almost impossible to judge in what position the wheelhead will be when the ball finally reaches the pockets.

Another casino advantage is the insensitivity of the new-type of track to wear or damage. Since, as the ball slows, it gradually recedes from the track wall, the point of departure is not nearly as well defined as for the old-type track. Thus, the drop-off point will remain more random, despite minor track irregularities. Bowl warpage, however, will adversely affect either type of ball track.

The Pocket Separators

Pocket separators, also called frets, are made of a nonmagnetic material such as brass, chrome-plated brass, or aluminum. A magnetic material, such as steel, cannot be used because rigging the wheel using a ball with a magnetized center is too easy. In most wheels, each individual fret is held in place with one or two small screws, accessible from the underside of the wheelhead.

In the newer "low-profile" wheels, the frets are lower, making the pockets shallower, as shown in Figure 6-4. This has the appearance of enhancing randomness by allowing the ball to jump over more pockets before landing. Although the increase in liveliness makes life harder for visual trackers and computer predictors, biases tend to be accentuated because the ball will visit a greater number of pockets before settling down.

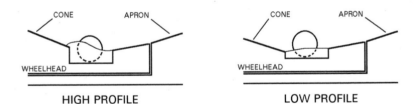

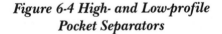

Figure 6-4 High- and Low-profile Pocket Separators

In some wheels, the entire circle of ball pockets is made from a single casting called a pocket ring. Such wheels are quite obvious; the ball pockets look like square cutouts in a circle of metal around the wheelhead. This not only eliminates the loose-fret problem, but in some wheels the pocket ring is independently adjustable, that is, it can be rotated relative to the circle of numbers. By rotating the pocket ring, any biases caused by particular pockets will be shifted to different numbers.

A few wheels have a moveable number ring, in which the entire ring of numbers can be repositioned in relation to the pockets. The effect is exactly the same as for the moveable pocket ring, except that this type of wheel is not as easy to spot.

The Number Sequences

As previously mentioned, the wheelhead number sequence is different for American wheels and French wheels. Both number sequences were illustrated earlier.

Since the design of all roulette wheels used today can be traced back to the first modern-era roulette wheel introduced by the Palais Royal in Paris about 1797, some people have wondered how two different number sequences developed. What we call the American number sequence is actually the order in which the numbers appeared on the first wheels at the Palais Royal. The original sequence, which had both a 0 and a 00, was probably devised by an employee of that venerable establishment.

This became the standard number sequence for almost a half century until Francois Blanc opened his casino in Homburg, Germany in 1843 and introduced the first single-zero roulette wheel. However, removing the 00 was not quite as simple as it first appeared because it resulted in two red numbers abutting, when the preferred pattern was to have alternating red and black numbers. Furthermore, they already knew about the center column "problem," in which a center column bet would cover a group of numbers clustered together on one side of the wheelhead.

With characteristic German perfectionism, these two deficiencies were enough reason to redesign the number sequence completely. The new sequence became the standard for single-zero wheels, which ultimately replaced all the double-zero wheels in Europe. Meanwhile, the obsolete double-zero wheels were being shipped to a new emerging market: the United States.

BIASED WHEELS: How They Get That Way

Biased roulette wheels are a fact of life. Casino management, however, would rather not discuss the subject and would lead you to believe that wheel bias is an extreme rarity. The casinos have good reason to play it down, since a biased wheel, if discovered by a player, can seriously cut into profits. One such example will be discussed and analyzed later, where the Gold Nugget, in Atlantic City, lost 3.8 million dollars. This is a major profit loss, even for a large, successful casino.

This chapter describes the various types of roulette wheel biases and the actual physical anomalies that cause a wheel to be non-random. These biases can be introduced accidentally or deliberately, or may simply be the result of long-term wear and tear.

A Sufficiently Random Wheel

For a roulette wheel to be random, it must be perfectly symmetrical, perfectly dimensioned, and perfectly balanced. In particular, the width and depth of every ball pocket must be identical, the pocket separators must be exactly the same height with the same stiffness, and the pocket pads must all have the same resilience. Furthermore, the ball track must be perfectly flat (unwarped) and circular, and must be smooth and uniform over its entire circumference. In the real world, such a wheel does not exist.

Even the finest-quality roulette wheels have built-in manufacturing tolerances and variances. The best that can be done is to manufacture a wheel that is "sufficiently random." This means that any bias unavoidably built into the wheel is not easily discernable and, in particular, is not strong enough to overcome the house advantage.

Not only should a wheel be sufficiently random when it is new, but it should be rugged enough to maintain that condition after years of continuous service. These are goals that are not always met, and when they are not met, it is usually not obvious. One reason for this is that randomness is not an easy characteristic to observe accurately or test for.

Even if a wheel is sufficiently random when it is new, as it ages it may develop irregularities causing it to exhibit non-random characteristics. Such irregularities may be the result of ordinary wear and tear, accidental damage, or deliberate tampering. Even small construction anomalies that are insignificant when the wheel is new, may eventually spawn certain non-random traits.

After a few years of heavy use, many wheels develop wear patterns that result in exploitable biases, especially if they have not been carefully maintained. These biases can usually be discovered by methodical and patient observation of the wheels while they are being played. When a wheel becomes biased, for whatever reason, it takes on special interest to the enterprising player.

Number Biases

Because of the counter-rotation of the ball and the wheelhead, many people think it is impossible for a roulette wheel to exhibit a preference for particular numbers. Although it usually happens accidentally, deliberately setting up a wheel to favor one or more contiguous groups of numbers is quite simple to do. A wheel can also be set up to favor black or red or odd or even.

Today, most wheel biases do occur accidentally, but sometimes a wheel is intentionally altered. If the bias is obvious, the casino will soon observe this and try to correct the problem. If it is subtle enough, casino personnel might never notice, and somebody has probably been working the wheel a long time for a small, but steady profit. These things can happen in several ways and here we will depict the most common causes of wheel bias.

Ball Drop

One useful trait of some older roulette wheels is the tendency of the ball drop-off point to be repetitive. That is, the ball has a strong tendency to repeatedly exit the ball track from the same place on the perimeter of the bowl. This can be caused by a slight warpage of the circular track or an almost-invisible wear-groove that guides the ball off the track at that point whenever it slows below a certain velocity.

In some cases, the track exit point is not as well defined or consistent, but is still useful for visual prediction work. In other cases, there may be more than one recurring exit point, which is a little harder to deal with. A wheel that is not perfectly level can exaggerate this type of bias.

Now, one would think that as soon as casino personnel observe the ball regularly exiting from the same point on the track, they would immediately remove the wheel from service and get it fixed. This is easier said than done. To demonstrate this, let me cite a personal experience.

Many years ago, a colleague and I were using his roulette wheel to do some predictability testing for a new computer program. It was a splendid old solid-wood wheel with a beautiful cherry finish. After a while we noticed that the ball regularly exited the track at two separate points, about 90 degrees apart. Since we were testing a program designed to work on relatively unbiased wheels, this was not a desirable situation, so we decided to try to fix it.

At first, we carefully located the two spots where the ball was exiting and examined that part of the track. We saw nothing, not even under magnification, and we could feel nothing with our fingers. Even though we could not identify any anomaly on the track, we tried to smooth and polish the two spots very carefully, but could not change the exiting characteristics. Finally, we tried tilting the wheel very slightly, but that only exaggerated the effect at one or the other of the two places.

All our efforts to fix the exiting problem failed and we finally concluded that the ball track had acquired a slight warp, invisible to the eye, but enough to cause the non-random characteristic to develop. If this wheel were in a casino, the casino would have the option of either scrapping the entire wheel or having it completely rebuilt. Most casinos would not bother, so long as the wheel is consistently earning money.

Why is a predictable exit point so important? Because to track a ball visually and determine what number span it is likely to end up in, three things need to be determined in advance: (1) The point on the perimeter of the track where the ball will exit, (2) when the ball will exit the track and (3) the position of the rotating wheelhead when it exits. If any of these three unknowns are eliminated, it changes visual prediction from an impossible task to a possible one. With a predictable exit point, a visual tracker will not only know *where* the ball will drop, but will also have a pretty good idea of *when* it will drop.

In a competent computer prediction program, determining the positions of the wheelhead and the ball at any given moment is not especially difficult. What *is* difficult to predict is when and where the ball will exit the track. In fact, enough error can easily be introduced in the exiting predictions to make the program ineffective. Knowing where the ball will exit, then, becomes a major advantage that can make a marginal program perform quite acceptably.

Pocket Separators

Occasionally a wheel may have one or more slightly-loose pocket separators (frets) between the ball pockets in the wheelhead. This may be the result of mishandling during wheel relocation and maintenance, or the wheel may have been deliberately rigged. Whatever the reason for the fret problem, the observant player may find it very beneficial.

A wheel with loosened frets will almost always favor certain numbers. When a lively ball strikes a loose fret, energy in the ball is absorbed by the movement of the fret, causing the ball to stop bouncing and land in a nearby pocket. The effect can get very strong if several adjacent frets are loose, but if the effect is too strong, casino personnel will eventually notice and have the wheel repaired. Loose frets are most effective with lively balls that skip around the wheelhead a lot, contacting a greater number of frets before finally coming to rest.

Pocket separators are usually made of brass, chrome-plated brass, or aluminum. In most wheels, each individual fret is held in place with one or two small screws, which are accessible from the underside of the wheelhead. In the newer "low-profile" wheels, the frets are lower, making the pockets shallower, which allows the ball to cross over more pockets before settling. The resultant increase in ball liveliness may frustrate visual trackers and computer predictors, but accentuates any bias caused by loose frets.

A fret can become loose by several means. It could happen by accident when a mechanic's wrench is dropped into the wheelhead and strikes a fret. Or it could happen deliberately by wiggling a fret with a pair of smooth-jaw pliers or striking it with a small hammer. A real pro would use a homemade tool with a slot that can be quickly slipped over a fret and twisted with some measure of precision. If done correctly, the loosened frets are not noticeable and can be hard to find, the amount of loosening being so slight that it can't be easily seen or felt.

The best method for finding loose frets is to move the wheel to a quiet location and tap each of the 38 frets with a hardwood implement, while listening for a difference in tone. This procedure takes time and patience, and is probably done very infrequently.

Occasionally, a fret may get damaged and have to be replaced. Finding an exact replacement is sometimes difficult, especially for an older wheel. If the replacement fret is not exactly the same height, the random characteristics of the wheel will be subverted. A slightly-high fret will catch the ball and favor the nearby pockets, whereas the ball will skip over a lower fret. If the replacement fret is a little thinner, the pockets on either side will be slightly wider, causing them to be favored.

Some manufacturers came up with a way to get around the fret problem: The entire circle of ball pockets is made from a single casting called a pocket ring. (The ball pockets in those wheels look like square cutouts in a circular metal casting around the wheelhead.) Although it is touted as eliminating loose frets, this construction probably has more to do with cost savings. Since it is a single-piece design, it eliminates 38 separate frets and associated mounting hardware, and greatly simplifies wheel assembly.

In some wheels the pocket ring is independently adjustable, that is, it can be rotated relative to the circle of numbers. By rotating the pocket ring, any biases caused by particular pockets will be shifted to different numbers. For example, if a wheel has a bias that favors the 8-12-29 number group, rotating the pocket ring clockwise by five numbers will change the number bias to 21-6-18. This could totally screw up anyone that has been clocking this wheel. The moveable ring could be a powerful countermeasure for wheel clockers if it were reset on a daily basis. However, since a wheel mechanic must perform the adjustment, it probably is not done more often than once a week, if that.

If you see a wheel that may have a moveable pocket ring, go ahead and clock it. Just be aware that if too much time passes between clocking and playing, the bias may have moved. Since resetting the pocket ring requires the wheel to be shut down for a short time, it is usually done early in the morning when the wheels are inactive. A good procedure, therefore, is to clock the wheel during the day shift and play the bias during the swing shift.

Some wheels have a moveable number ring, in which the ring of numbers is repositioned instead of the pockets. This type of wheel is not as obvious and is rarely found in the United States.

Pocket Pads

The pocket pads, that is, the material at the bottoms of the ball pockets in the wheelhead can be quite a range of substances. In the older wheels, it is usually a soft vinyl material that is cemented in place. Except for the 0 and 00, the vinyl is colored red and black in alternating pockets. In some wheels the pads are a green or blue felt material. Many of the newer wheel designs, have pocket bottoms with a hard plastic surface, which imparts a greater bounce to the ball.

When pads have to be replaced because they have become worn or damaged, it needs to be done with diligent care. Often the replacement pad material does not match the thickness and resiliency of the original and sometimes the mechanic is not meticulous enough in applying an even layer of cement. This can create trapped-air pockets under the pad that can modify the resiliency characteristics.

If the resilience of the pads is not identical in all the pockets, the wheel will lose its random characteristics. A softer, non-resilient pad will absorb energy from the ball and tend to retain it in the pocket. A harder, highly-resilient pad will tend to kick the ball out of that pocket. In most roulette wheels the pads are somewhere between the two extremes.

Casinos and their wheel mechanics do not usually pay too much attention to the pocket pads, not realizing that an easy way to rig a wheel is to manipulate the pads. A wheel can be made to favor or disfavor certain numbers or colors by changing some pads to a material with different resilience.

Wheel Leveling

At one time, if a visual tracker found a wheel that was a good candidate for prediction work except that the ball drop was too random, it was a simple matter to fix by slipping a matchbook under one of the leveling feet. Since all wheels have three or four leveling feet, at least one of them was always accessible to a person standing next to the wheel. Even when it was clearly visible from the player's side of the table, nobody paid any attention to the matchbook, because it just looked as if it was inadvertently pushed under the edge of the wheel. Of course, the introduction of plexiglass security shields put an end to such shenanigans.

Even without the help of a matchbook, a roulette wheel is often not exactly level. This is usually due to an uneven table. Every time a roulette wheel is repositioned on a table or moved to another table, it should be re-leveled. This is not always done. Although leveling is one of the easiest things to check on a roulette wheel, many casinos are rather unconcerned about it, probably because they do not really understand what difference it makes. This is good for some players and bad for the casinos.

It is good for the players because a roulette wheel that is off level by as little as 1/8 inch will magnify any non-randomness in the ball drop characteristic. That is, a tendency for the ball to drop repeatedly into the wheelhead from the same area on the perimeter of the track, will be strengthened. If the tilt is even more pronounced, a random ball drop can be turned into a non-random drop.

Obviously, a non-random ball drop is a major advantage for visual trackers. In fact, if the ball drop is completely random, prediction by visual tracking is impossible to accomplish. Additionally, a non-random ball drop simplifies the programming and improves the accuracy of a computer prediction system.

BIASED WHEELS: How to Find Them

As we saw in the previous chapter, a roulette wheel can become biased in many ways. For a wheel that is in service for two shifts a day, in one month the ball will have circled the track more than 50,000 times and the wheelhead will have turned well over 50,000 revolutions. After a few months of this kind of wear and tear, any wheel that does not start to lose its random characteristics would be very unusual. No matter how well it is constructed, after a few years of service, with millions of ball spins and millions of wheelhead revolutions, a wheel would have to be made out of Kryptonite to retain its original random characteristics.

There are, and will continue to be, plenty of biased roulette wheels available. There are more than 3,000 roulette wheels in legal casinos around the world, over 600 of them in the United States, so if you cannot find a biased wheel, you are not really trying. Or, maybe, you don't know the best ways to go about locating them. That is what this chapter is about.

Clocking Wheel

Clocking is the term used for collecting and recording the winning numbers as they occur on a roulette wheel. It is the basic technique used for determining if the wheel is biased. How is this accomplished? Usually with a pencil and paper and lots of patience. Will the casino ask you to cease and desist? Not likely.

For example, if you are writing down numbers while seated at a roulette table, they should not care so long as you also keep laying down your bets. If you start winning big, they will wonder what kind of system you are using. If you continue winning, they *may* ask you to stop writing down numbers. I say "may" because there is always the fear that such a request might cause you to cash in your chips and leave. The only people that casinos worry about more than big winners are big winners that pick up their money and go home.

If you are not playing, you can write down numbers all night long and they will probably ignore you. Whatever you do, do not get so apprehensive that you devise some kind of hidden device for recording the numbers surreptitiously. This can get you into serious trouble. Just use a pen or pencil and a small pocket notebook. Keep in mind that there is no law against wheel clocking, but do not get arrogant; always try to maintain a low profile.

Many casinos have a routine where each roulette wheel is rotated a small amount, typically, 1/8 turn every week. They do this primarily to redistribute the wear on the ball track and to avoid developing a groove on the side where the dealer releases the ball. To confuse wheel clockers, some casinos also move wheels from table to table, usually on a monthly basis.

Therefore, when you start clocking a wheel, try to identify it, and its position on the table, as explicitly as possible. To do this, you should inspect the wheel meticulously for any individualistic characteristics and record them in your notebook. This is not so easy in a casino where all the wheels are the same make and model, so you have to look carefully for flaws such as scratches in the finish, wear patterns, or discolorations. Then, if you return to that table more than one shift later, be sure that the wheel characteristics match.

When you start to record the winning numbers, write them down in order of occurrence and try not to miss any. Professional clockers typically collect at least 400 numbers before making a preliminary decision as to whether or not the wheel has possibilities. If it appears to be biased, they will collect another 800 to 1000 numbers for verification. These people, however, have to be conservative because when they sit down to play a biased wheel, large sums of money are at risk.

Because we will use a more statistical approach in assessing the data, 150 to 200 winning numbers should be adequate for the initial evaluation. If the data looks good, go back and collect 300 to 400 more. This is not as tedious as it sounds. Typically, a roulette wheel in the United States is spun 100 to 120 times per hour, thus, it should take one to two hours to collect the initial data and less than four hours to verify it. Six hours of your time is a small price to pay to be able to play a wheel that will make you a sure winner.

Actually, it's not quite that simple. In order to find a potentially-biased wheel, you may have to collect initial data for many wheels. But then, nobody said getting rich is easy.

Clocking Multiple Wheels

There is a major shortcut that can make clocking less tedious. In some places it is possible to clock more than one wheel at the same time. If you find a casino that has two or three wheels in the same pit, or grouped closely together, there is no reason that you cannot stroll around and clock all of them simultaneously. Just be careful that you do not mix them up in your notebook.

All of the new casinos and more of the old casinos are installing electronic display boards, which they call reader boards. These boards display the last sixteen or twenty-one (depending on the model) winning numbers. Each time a new number wins, it is displayed on top and the oldest number scrolls off the bottom of the board. Reader boards are made-to-order for wheel clockers. Not only can you clock more wheels simultaneously, but I even noticed one situation where you could see the numbers on three boards while seated at a bar stool. How good can it get?

One caution on reader boards: Although they are generally quite dependable, an occasional one will malfunction. This is usually in the form of displaying a spurious repeat number, which is probably caused by a misaligned sensor unit. If you see a board with repeat numbers, watch the wheel for a while and verify that the numbers are actually repeating. An excellent practice is to monitor any wheel you are clocking for 15 or 20 spins before depending entirely on the reader board.

Clocking can get very boring, especially if you are in a casino with only one or two wheels. To while away the time, you could collect the numbers while you are playing your favorite betting system on the wheel. Sometimes, this may be the best procedure and your system play could result in a profit whether or not the wheel is biased.

Identifying a Biased Wheel

Once a sufficient amount of data is collected for a particular wheel, it has to be evaluated to establish whether it reveals any biases. The place to start would be to determine which numbers in the data set have the highest frequency of occurrence. The probability of a particular number winning is 1 chance out of 38 (on an American wheel), or once every 38 spins, on the average. Since the most prevalent number in the data would be occurring more often than the average, the question is: What frequency of occurrence would be considered outside the normal range for a random wheel?

The answer to that question gets us into statistical areas such as significance tests and confidence levels. Let us avoid that if we can, but it would still be nice to have some guideline as a basis for deciding whether or not the initial data suggests that it is worth pursuing further.

The empirical rule that we recommend is: If a number wins ten or more times in 200 spins *and* both adjacent numbers also exceed the average (for an American wheel) of 5.3 wins per 200 spins, you should get really interested in that wheel. For instance, if in 200 spins, the number 17 wins eleven times, this would not be significant unless the numbers 5 and 32 won at least seven times each. There is a good reason for this.

Since the probability of winning is 1/38, then the winning number would be expected to occur 2.63 percent of the time. A num-

ber that wins 10 times out of 200 spins is occurring 5 percent of
the time (10/200 = 0.05), or almost twice the expected rate. That
alone is nothing to rave about. In fact, if the number won twice
that often, it still could be a random characteristic. However, if
the adjacent numbers on both sides were also winning more often than the expected probability, we *might* be looking at a normal curve.

The *normal curve* was devised in 1733 by Abraham de Moivre, a
French mathematician, in the course of supplementing his income
by analyzing games of chance for wealthy gamblers. It is a bell-
shaped curve that can mathematically represent many different
kinds of data and is particularly applicable to numerous gambling
situations.

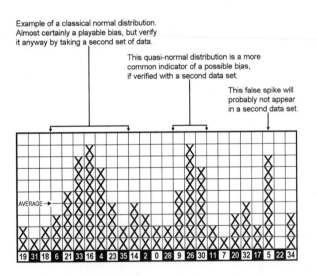

Figure 8-1 Frequency Distribution Plot

An example of a frequency distribution plot is shown in Figure 8-
1. This example (which spans about two-thirds of an American
wheel) illustrates the difference between a normal curve, a quasi-
normal curve, and a random spike. Random spikes are not likely

to be caused by wheel bias and will probably not be replicated in the verification data. Any plot that looks similar to the bell shape of a normal curve, however, has serious possibilities. To determine this, the data should always be plotted on a frequency distribution chart.

Figures 8-2 and 8-3 are blank frequency distribution charts for American and French wheels. Although the entire contents of this book are copyrighted, you are hereby given permission to make copies of these charts for your personal use.

The best way to apply the charts is to first collect a set of data in a small notebook. Then find a quiet corner and transfer each set of data to a chart. Keep in mind that the chart is a linear representation of a round wheel and that the right end connects to the left end.

To determine the average wins for any wheel number in a given data set, divide the number of data points by 38 (37 for a French wheel). For instance, if you have 230 data points, the average will be about 6 wins per number. In this case, draw a line or make a mark on the chart six boxes from the bottom. By doing this, you can easily tell which wheel numbers are exceeding the average, and by how much.

Next, analyze the frequency distribution plot and look for a pattern that resembles a normal or a quasi-normal curve. If the central number is at least double the average and the numbers on either side of the central number both exceed the average, go get another set of data on that wheel—it has distinct possibilities. If the second data set exhibits a similar normal curve, you have almost certainly hit pay dirt.

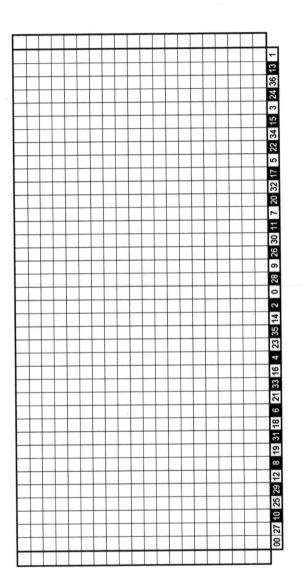

Figure 8-2 Clocking Chart for American Double-Zero Wheel

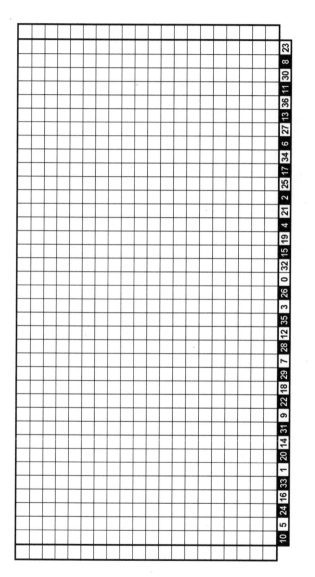

Figure 8-3 Clocking Chart for French Single-Zero Wheel

A truly-random wheel (if there is such a thing) can easily come up with winning number sequences that will absolutely convince you that it is biased. However, it will rarely duplicate the same phony bias in two separate data-collecting sessions. This is why the verification process is so important. If the second set of data shows a similar bias, then the wheel is probably worth playing. Once you have determined that a particular wheel is biased, it is always worthwhile to triple check by collecting and evaluating a third set of data, before risking your money.

If you question the prevalence of biased roulette wheels and think this chapter was pie-in-the-sky, think about it again after reading the next chapter in which we describe how $3.8 million was won at a major casino in Atlantic City.

BIASED WHEELS:
A Case Study

One fine summer day in Atlantic City, a gambler seated himself at a roulette wheel in the Golden Nugget and started to place bets. He bet $2000 straight-up on each of five numbers and continued to bet the same five numbers spin after spin. Almost from the start, one or another of these numbers seemed to hit at a higher-than-expected rate and he began to win at a steady pace.

As his winnings began to accumulate, he attracted a sizeable crowd. Over the next two days he played approximately 18 hours, never varying his bet—always those same five numbers. When he finally quit, he had won a total of $3.8 million and generously left a $25,000 tip for the dealers. The year was 1986 and this achievement was an all-time record win for any roulette player in a legal casino.

When the incident was reported in the press, most people assumed it was a hoax or a public relations stunt. It was neither. The Golden Nugget really lost the money.

The rest of the story is that the roulette player was a known gambler from Nevada by the name of William T. Walters, more familiarly known as Billy Walters. When he first walked into the casino, he placed two million dollars on deposit and requested a private game at the roulette wheel of his choice, with no betting limits—not an unusual arrangement for high rollers. Part of the agreement was that the casino could not bring in new dealers and that he could play all weekend without the casino closing the wheel. Golden Nugget management went along with these terms because they assumed that sooner or later they would be two million dollars richer.

Although the Golden Nugget has single-zero wheels available, Walters selected a particular double-zero wheel. At 5.26 percent vigorish, the casino was certain it could not lose. In two days they found out how wrong they were.

The moment Walters was finished playing, the casino shut down the roulette table and began an extensive investigation. The wheel was removed from the casino floor and was inspected and tested by casino personnel as well as outside experts. No anomalies could be found. It was also examined by New Jersey Gaming Control inspectors, who found the wheel to be in compliance with legal requirements. To this day, the wheel has been kept locked up and has never been used again.

All the roulette wheels at the Golden Nugget were the older style deep-pocket type. Within weeks, the wheels were all replaced with an English-made low-profile type in an attempt to prevent a recurrence of such a financial disaster. Not long after this event, the Golden Nugget was purchased by Bally Resorts and renamed *The Grand*.

A Biased Wheel

The five magic numbers played by Billy Walters were 7, 10, 20, 27 and 36. Those numbers are probably seared into the brain of the casino manager and the brains of several pit bosses and shift managers. Localizing these numbers on an American wheelhead reveals that they consist of two pairs, 7-20 and 10-27, with the 36 found between the pairs. The five numbers cover a total span width of 16 numbers—less than half the circumference of the wheelhead.

Although many people were scratching their heads, the real experts knew that this could have happened for only one reason: the wheel was biased. Obviously, the wheel exhibited a bimodal bias in that it favored two separate pairs of numbers. What about the lone 36? It might have been a decoy to confuse the casino personnel, but with bets of $2000 a number, that is unlikely. Billy Walters was trying to win the money as fast as possible, which for a one-shot operation, is the best course of action. However, unless someone we know clocked the actual event, we can never be sure.

Why can we be so certain that this was a biased wheel? For four very solid reasons:

1. Whenever a wheel repeatedly favors the same numbers it is, by definition, biased.

2. If prediction techniques were used, such as visual tracking or computer assistance, different numbers would have been bet for every spin.

3. Walters selected a particular double-zero wheel, when he could have played a single-zero wheel with a much lower house advantage.

4. Walters is known to have a team that clocks wheels, trying to find biases. Apparently his team did its job well.

A Mathematical Analysis

Now that we know with certainty that the wheel was biased, why do we need to analyze the situation any further? Because, it is often assumed that any bias too subtle for the casino personnel to notice, would be too weak or inconsistent to be profitable.

Clearly, the casino management at the Golden Nugget was totally unaware that one of their roulette wheels was seriously biased, yet a large sum of money was won in a short time. For anyone interested in roulette wheel bias, an analysis of this event can provide important information as to how much bias is, or is not, obvious to the casino.

With the information available to us, the only practical way to do a mathematical analysis is to back into it, starting with the total winnings. The net amount won by Walters was $3.8 million and, over a span of 38 hours, his actual playing time was 18 hours.

Dividing $3.8 million by 18 hours, gives an average profit of $211,111 per hour.

Before arriving at any meaningful results, however, we need to estimate how much money was actually put at risk to win the $3.8 million. Since Walters and an associate of his were the only players at that table, it can be assumed that the ball was spun somewhere between 90 and 120 times each hour. After performing some empirical calculations, it turns out that an average rate of 105.556 spins per hour results in the simplest numbers and is probably a reasonable estimate.

Multiplying 18 hours by 105.556 gives 1900, the total number of spins for the entire session. Now, dividing the net winnings of $3.8 million by 1900 spins gives us $2000, which is Walters' average profit per spin. At each spin of the ball, Walters bet $2000 on each of the five numbers for a total risk of $10,000.

The player's advantage can now be calculated from these numbers, which is his profit as a percent of the total risk:

$$\text{Player's Advantage} = \frac{2000}{10000} \times 100 = 20 \text{ percent}$$

This is a whopping advantage. Considering that he also had to overcome the house edge of 5.26 percent, this is even more impressive.

What we really want to know, however, is how obvious the wheel bias was to an interested observer. Since Walters bet $10,000 on each spin of the ball, his total risk was $10,000 times 1900 spins, which comes out to $19 million for the entire session. To net a profit of $3.8 million, he would have had to win $19 million plus $3.8 million, or a total of $22.8 million.

Each time one of his numbers hit, he won 35 times $2000 and got back his original $2000 bet on that number, for a total return of

$72,000. Dividing $72,000 into the $22.8 million total winnings will give the number of wins in 1900 spins:

$$\text{Actual Wins in 1900 Spins} = \frac{\$22,800,000}{\$72,000} = 317$$

As we explained earlier, for a truly-random double-zero wheel, the probability of a particular number winning is 1/38, or 1 chance out of every 38 spins. Then the probability of any one of five particular numbers winning is 5/38, and the expected number of wins in 1900 spins for a random wheel would be:

$$\text{Expected Wins in 1900 Spins} = \frac{5}{38} \times 1900 = 250$$

Mr. Walters obviously beat the statistical probability by a nice margin. With a total of 1900 spins and 317 actual wins, simple division tells us that one or another of his five numbers hit an average of every 6 spins. Then each individual number won one-fifth of the time, or an average of every 30 spins. Since it is unlikely that each of the five numbers had exactly the same bias strength, at least one or two of those numbers had to show up more often than once every 30 spins. Yet, the casino did not realize that the wheel was seriously biased.

Evaluating the Event

Question: Before Billy Walters showed up, would an alert observer have noticed that a few numbers were coming up an *average* of every 30 spins instead of every 38 spins? Not necessarily.

Let's say you had been watching a wheel for about 30 spins and saw the same number come up three times. This may have gotten your attention, but when the number did not show up again for another 60 spins, you forgot about it. Unless you had a calculator built into your brain, you probably would not realize that the number was still winning on a long-term average of every 30 spins.

Question: Instead of an independent observer, wouldn't a casino employee be more likely to notice that 30-spin bias?

Almost no chance at all, especially in a large casino. Floor supervisors and pit bosses have better things to do than clock a roulette wheel. I have seen a floor person clocking a wheel on only three or four occasions. They usually stick with it for twenty or thirty minutes and then show the list of numbers to the pit boss. The pit boss must have always been satisfied because they never continued the clocking. So long as their wheels are profitable, most pit bosses are more concerned with past posting than with bias.

Of course, if the wheel is so biased that it would be apparent after only thirty minutes of clocking, the casino would already be bankrupt. In a thirty minute period, the ball is spun about 50 times. Can anyone spot a 30-spin bias in 50 spins? Hardly!

If a 30-spin bias is so hard to spot, yet capable of winning millions, what about a 32- or 34-spin bias? For anyone that is happy to win at a slower rate, there have to be plenty of wheels with 32- to 34-spin biases out there. Just remember, for a wheel with a 36-spin bias, the house edge has dropped to zero. Any stronger bias than that, and the player is a winner (over the long run).

Finally, a very interesting sidelight to this event is the fact that New Jersey Gaming Control inspectors found the Golden Nugget roulette wheel to be in full compliance and that other experts could find nothing wrong with it. This shows that a careful visual and mechanical inspection of a wheel will not necessarily reveal a strong bias. The only sure way to find a bias is to clock the wheel over a long period of time, which is a rather tedious chore. Nevertheless, even clocking may not always tell the story, because some biases show up only at certain wheelhead speeds.

If you think that the Golden Nugget event was a fluke, consider that almost exactly three years later, the Billy Walters team of clockers entered the Claridge in Atlantic City and spent four days *overtly* clocking all eight wheels in the casino. On the fifth day,

Billy Walters and his associates sat down at one of the wheels and won $200,000 in a period of eight hours. Three days later, after the Claridge had all their wheels inspected, tested, and serviced, the team of clockers returned for another four days of intensive clocking. Shortly thereafter, Billy Walters and his associates reappeared and won another $300,000 on a second wheel.

The roulette wheels at the Claridge were old-style deep-pocket models manufactured in the United States. Shortly after this incident, those casinos in Atlantic City that had not already done so, purchased new low-profile wheels, most of them manufactured by John Huxley of London. If you look around Las Vegas, however, you can find many casinos that still use the deep-pocket models. Go figure.

PREDICTION BY VISUAL TRACKING

Visual tracking is a time-honored method for predicting the outcome at a roulette wheel, and it is perfectly legal. Good visual trackers are, understandably, proud of their talent. To be a proficient tracker takes a sharp eye and practice, practice, practice. The casinos do not like visual trackers, but then, they do not like anyone that wins consistently.

What is visual tracking anyway? It is the act of carefully observing a spinning roulette ball and its positional relationship to the counter-rotating wheelhead in order to predict into what sector of the wheelhead the ball will most likely fall. If you question that anyone can do this successfully, read on. Most people do not have the necessary patience, visual acuity, and concentration to be successful trackers. For someone who does have these abilities (and they will not know until they try), the information in this chapter will provide the basic techniques to get them started. It is a skill that can be utilized whenever one runs into a suitable wheel, which can easily happen while scouting for biased wheels.

Playing Conditions
Although an accomplished tracker can deal with a variety of conditions, to assure any degree of success, the beginner needs to find exactly the right situation. So much as possible, the wheel and the dealer should have the following distinctions:
1. The wheel should be an old model with the old-type ball track.
2. A repetitive ball drop occurring at the same point on the perimeter of the ball track at least half the time.
3. A dealer who always spins the ball reasonably fast, and maintains a steady wheelhead rotation at a moderate speed—no faster than two seconds per revolution.

4. A ball without excessive liveliness that tends to stay within five or six pockets from where it originally enters the wheelhead.

Although the above items are listed in order of importance, for a beginner with any hope of success, all the items are mandatory. Ball drop-off repetition can be determined on any wheel after observing four or five spins. If the ball drop-off point is not repetitive, go to the next wheel unless you are also clocking for bias.

Proper tracking, requires a good view of the ball track and the wheelhead. The best position for this is to stand right up to the wheel (do not lean on the plexiglass), just next to the last seat. If you stand squarely in front of the wheel or toward the corner of the table, you are more likely to be jostled and your associate will not have as good a view of your signals. Yes, you will have to work with an associate who does the actual betting, because you will not be in a very good position to do so.

The best place for your associate is at the back of the table, next to the dealer. This position affords her the best view of you and easy access to the center-column bet. If that position is not open, the next best place is at the far end of the table. You should establish a subtle, but unmistakable signaling system.

The Mechanics of Tracking

In the following discussion of tracking, it will be assumed that the wheelhead is rotating counter-clockwise and the ball is spun in a clockwise direction. In North American casinos, this is true 98 percent of the time at a right-handed roulette table (a table where the wheel is to the right of the dealer). At a left-handed table, the dealer will often spin the ball counter-clockwise and the wheel clockwise. Occasionally you may encounter a European-trained dealer who reverses the wheelhead and ball rotation after every spin, provided the pit boss allows her to do that. Unless you are an accomplished tracker, avoid such a situation.

We will start by using the single zero on the wheelhead as the reference point for reasons to be explained later. The eye must

constantly follow that zero reference point as the wheelhead rotates. The ball, rotating in the opposite direction, will be seen, in
peripheral vision, as a white blur every time it passes the zero.

Never focus on the ball; keep your eyes focused on the rotating
zero. Reversing the process usually does not work. Unless the
wheelhead is turning very slowly, for your peripheral vision to
catch the passing of the green zero is difficult to do while your
eyes are focused on the ball—and you must keep track of both.

A fixed reference point on the bowl must be selected so that you
know when the wheelhead has traveled one revolution. The point
should be on the apron between the ball track and the pockets,
and should be at the opposite side of the bowl from where you
are standing so that it can be easily seen. A line on the apron or
one of the ball deflectors is a good choice. See Figure 10-1.

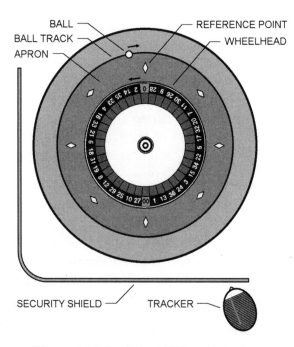

Figure 10-1 Position of Visual Tracker

Most of the time, when the dealer first launches the ball it travels several revolutions for every full revolution of the wheelhead. It is not hard to visualize that during one wheelhead revolution, the ball will cross the zero reference point several times. In fact, the number of crossings provides an accurate measure of the ratio of wheelhead speed to ball speed.

If the ball is moving five times as fast as the wheelhead, six crossings will occur during one revolution, 60 degrees apart. As the ball slows, the crossings will drift in a counter-clockwise direction and get farther apart until one crossing occurs about every 90 degrees. This counter-clockwise drift of the crossings will continue until a point is reached where there are two crossings, about 180 degrees apart. When that occurs, the ball and the wheelhead are moving at the same speed. As the ball continues to slow, it will be moving at a lower speed than the wheelhead. True, the wheelhead is also slowing, but its rate of deceleration is so much less than that of the ball that it can be safely ignored.

It should not be hard to visualize that two crossings are the smallest number possible with two counter-rotating objects. Consequently, when the ball starts to slow below the wheelhead speed, the crossings will begin to drift in a clockwise direction and their number will begin to increase. By the time the ball has slowed to one-half of the wheelhead speed, there will be three crossings, 120 degrees apart. However, if the wheelhead is rotating at a leisurely speed, the ball may never slow this much before dropping off the track.

So far, we have been talking in terms of degrees, where the wheel is visualized as a 360-degree circle. Most wheels have eight ball deflectors located on the apron below the ball track. Consequently, most trackers find it easier to divide the wheel into eight sectors, using the deflectors as reference points. Then the span between any two deflectors is 1/8 of the wheel perimeter and a span of two sectors is equal to 90 degrees. The following table summarizes the zero-ball crossings, showing the distance between crossings in both degrees and sectors:

Crossings In One W/H Revolution	Crossing Drift Direction	Degrees Between Crossings	Sectors Between Crossings	W/H-Ball Speed Ratio
8	CCW	45	1	1:7
6	CCW	60	1-1/3	1:5
4	CCW	90	2	1:3
3	CCW	120	2-2/3	1:2
2	None	180	4	1:1
3	CW	120	2-2/3	2:1
4	CW	90	2	3:1

The only moment when the zero-ball crossing is not in motion is when the ball is moving at exactly the same speed (in the opposite direction) as the wheelhead. When the ball is moving faster than the wheelhead, the crossing drifts in a counter-clockwise direction. As the ball slows down below the wheelhead speed, the crossing drift stops and then begins to move in a clockwise direction. Except for that moment when both the ball and wheelhead speeds are the same, the crossing always appears to be in motion.

The main purpose of this section was to show that a visual correlation exists between the movement of the wheelhead and the ball, and how to track it. During the early part of the ball's spin, this visual link is only of academic interest. For the last few revolutions, however, it is the primary tool used by the tracker as an aid in predicting where the ball will land.

Judging The Ball Drop

Even after carefully selecting playable roulette wheels, from one wheel to the next, the wheelhead may be rotating faster or slower; the ball may drop off the track at a slower/faster speed because it is smaller/larger or lighter/heavier; the repetitive drop-off point may be narrow or broad, or it may be bimodal. The one thing that is certain is that every situation will be different.

For purposes of this discussion, we are going to assume a particular set of conditions. In our hypothetical wheel, the sections are mentally numbered from one to eight in a clockwise direction, and the wheelhead reference point is the deflector at the left side of Section 1. A single repetitive drop-off point occurs in Sector 6. The wheelhead is moving moderately fast and the speed of the ball at the time of drop-off is about 1/2 the speed of the wheelhead.

Under these ideal conditions, there are just two variables that the tracker has to predetermine: (1) The revolution during which the ball drops off the track, and (2) The position of the wheelhead when the ball drops.

Judging the revolution during which the ball will drop is simply an estimate of ball speed, which can be done in one of two ways. The first way is a direct observation of how far the ball slows before it drops off the track. After watching several spins of the ball, some people can accurately judge when the ball is about to drop. Actually, it is a little more difficult than that because the judgement has to be made three revolutions in advance. That is, the determination has to be that at a certain point in time the ball will drop after three more turns.

The disadvantage of this method is that it is not easy to do while focussed on the rotating zero. The advantage is that it is independent of the wheelhead speed.

The second method is to gauge the distance between zero-ball crossings continuously. As the ball slows, the distance will get smaller and smaller, providing a good estimate of ball speed, assuming the wheelhead speed is consistent from spin to spin. The advantage of this method is that the eyes can remain fixed on the zero. The disadvantage is that it is highly dependent on a consistent wheelhead speed.

Placing The Bet

The final five or six revolutions of the ball are when the tracker really has to concentrate. Most dealers cut off betting when the ball is within one or two turns of the drop-off point. Thus, the tracker needs to signal her confederate when the ball is no closer than two to three turns, to allow enough time for placing the bet.

Even the best trackers cannot judge the ball drop more accurately than to within a spread of 12 to 14 numbers. Thus, the center column bet on the American wheel, which includes most of the pockets within a total spread of 15 numbers, is made to order. This bet covers the span (clockwise) from 23 to 5, with five gaps (0, 7, 9, 28 and 30) and only two numbers outside the span. Understandably, it is the most common bet placed by visual tracking teams.

It can be seen in Figure 10-2 that the single zero is three pockets counter-clockwise from 26, which is the number in the middle of the center-column span. The green zero, being much easier to follow visually than the 26, is used as the tracking reference for the center-column bet. The tracker just remembers that the true reference is about 2/3 of a sector behind the wheelhead rotation.

This is fine if the ball is predicted to land near the middle of the center-column span. What if the ball appears to be heading for a section completely outside the center-column span? The bettor should then place a minimum bet on one or both of the other columns. If the tracking team has become fairly adept, the bettor could use one or more of the contiguous number combinations described earlier.

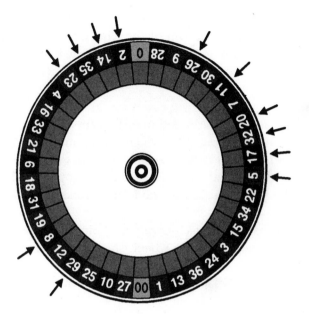

Figure 10-2 Numbers Covered
by Center Column Bet

Visual Tracking Aids

The main reason that casinos do not like visual trackers is that, historically, many trackers have been opportunists. In the days before plexiglass screens were used, people would often crowd around and lean on the rim of the wheel. If a tracker could see that the ball was not going to drop where the bet was placed, she would flick a finger over the edge of the bowl, knocking the ball off the race.

This is not as obvious an action as it seems. In fact, it is far less obvious than switching balls, which is what magnetic scam artists had to do to get an iron-core ball into the game. However, the plexiglass screens that are placed around almost all roulette wheels today, have pretty well eliminated these tricks.

This leaves past posting as the scam of choice. Because the tracker's eyes are constantly on the wheel, she knows before the dealer where the ball is about to fall. Whenever the tracker and bettor have a sufficiently-elaborate set of signals, this is a perfect setup for past posting.

Past posting is not a recommended procedure for the reader. As explained elsewhere, the penalties for getting caught can be severe. If you decide to try your hand (or eye) at visual tracking, play it safe and do it honestly.

THE CLASSICAL SYSTEMS

Apart from the various prediction techniques described in this book, a non-biased roulette wheel can be played in only two ways. The first way is the "hunch" method, which may be the digits in your daughter's birthday, the latest winning lotto numbers, or just your personal "lucky" numbers. Whatever the justification, there is no scientific or analytical reason for selecting these numbers—they are just based on a hunch. Most Americans use the "hunch" method when playing roulette.

The second way is the "system" method. In Europe, most roulette players use a mathematical system and consider hunch players to be fools who will soon be parted from their money. The system player believes that roulette should be approached methodically, using some sort of numerical or logical basis. European casinos act nonchalant and cater to this mentality by providing note pads and pencils at the roulette table. Of course, when a system player starts winning consistently, the casino managers tend to lose their composure.

Mathematical betting systems have received a bad rap because of the large number of people that have lost money trying to play them. Of course, the main reason they lose is that they have not learned or practiced the fine points of system play, which makes the difference between winning and losing. Although the casinos perpetuate the myth that a mathematical system cannot win consistently and try to act unconcerned, most of them dread an intelligent and knowledgeable systems player.

If there is even a single system that consistently works, why isn't everyone playing roulette and beating the house? Some are. However, most people do not take the time and effort to learn how to do things properly and wonder why they always lose. Just look at what happened to the game of blackjack after Dr. Thorp published his method for beating it in 1962. The popularity of blackjack soared and the casinos, after some initial concerns, installed more tables and earned more money than they ever did before. Yes, there are people who beat blackjack regularly, just as there are people who beat roulette. Those few consistent winners, however, are so heavily swamped out by the hordes of losers that they have little effect on the overall casino profits.

This chapter will describe in some detail how the major classical roulette betting systems are intended to work. At first glance, they all appear to be quite foolproof, but each of them has limitations and pitfalls that need to be fully understood and compensated for. Consequently, playing the systems exactly as they are depicted in this chapter is not recommended. The next chapter covers the adjustments and fine points that most people never learn, but which are required to make the systems perform profitably. Before jumping to the next chapter, however, it is recommended that you first acquire an understanding of the basic systems.

Most roulette betting systems are designed around the even-money bets, which are the six bets along the outside of the roulette betting layout. They are: red, black, even, odd, low (1-18), and high (19-36). On an unbiased wheel, all of these bets are monetarily and statistically equivalent, so keep in mind that, from a systems standpoint, it makes no difference which one of the six is being played.

The Martingales

The Martingale and its variations are the most popular and best-known betting systems in the world. Also known as doubling-up or progression systems, they are praised by those who have won big and damned by those who have lost their shirts. There is no question that they can produce either result. The basic Martingale principle, which can be applied to any repetitive even-money wager, was devised at least three hundred years ago and its popularity has never waned.

As with most roulette betting systems, this one is applied to the even-money outside bets, defined before. In its most fundamental form, the amount of the initial bet is doubled after each successive loss. After each win, the bet is reduced to its initial value and remains there until the next loss occurs. In this way, all losses are eventually recovered with a net gain of the amount of the initial bet.

For instance, if an initial bet of 5 units is lost, the next bet would be doubled to 10 units. If the second bet also lost, the third bet would be 20 units; if the third bet lost, the fourth bet would be 40 units, and so forth. Whenever any bet is won, the next bet is reduced to the initial amount of 5 units.

The danger in this system is that eventually a long string of successive losses will keep increasing the amount of the bet until it reaches the table limit. At many roulette wheels, the table limit for outside bets is set to 200 times the minimum bet. This ratio will allow seven consecutive bet doublings before the table limit is encountered. At a table with a 1000 unit limit, starting with 5 units, a continuous string of losses will look like this:

5	10	20	40	80	160	320	640

After the eighth loss, the next doubling will encounter the table limit.

Eight losses in a row for an even-money bet is not as rare an occurrence as one might think. On average, it will happen once every 170 spins of the ball. In most U.S. casinos, a roulette ball is typically spun 80 to 100 times every hour. Consequently, for a particular even-money bet one can expect such a losing streak to occur at least once every two hours on any given wheel.

The classical Martingale is obviously not for everyone, especially if we start talking in terms of dollars instead of the innocuous "units." After seven straight losses, the idea of risking an additional 640 dollars in an attempt to recoup the 635 dollars already lost, and ending up with a five-dollar profit is ludicrous to most people, especially, since the statistics show that this situation could occur every couple of hours.

Table Limits

For many years, gambling industry experts and consultants such as John Scarne have advised casinos to "protect" themselves from systems players by maintaining tight table limits. As a result, most casinos have kept the minimum-to-maximum bet ratio at their roulette tables to no greater than 100 to 1, or, at most, 200 to 1, thus limiting the number of bet doublings to six or seven.

Detractors of progressive betting systems such as the Martingale usually cite the casino table limits as the main obstacle to preventing these systems from being successful. This is really not so. The main obstacle is the ineptness of the average system player. The accomplished system player has always known of methods that compensate for low table limits, methods that will be presented in the next chapter.

Recently, more and more casinos have dramatically increased the maximum bet limits, probably because they finally figured out that they can't really get hurt. After a long string of losses, most Martingale players run out of money or get cold feet before they encounter the table limit. Raising the limit has a minimal effect on the proficient player and simply allows the inept players to lose more.

Today, some of the most profitable Las Vegas strip casinos have posted minimum bet limits of $3 to $5 and maximum limits of $10,000 to $20,000, for outside bets. We are talking eleven or twelve bet doublings. Obviously, they are not worried.

The Grand Martingale

The Grand Martingale, sometimes called the Great Martingale, is probably the most popular variation on the basic Martingale system. After every loss, in addition to doubling the bet, one more unit is added. If a bet of 5 units is lost, the next bet will be 11 instead of 10 units, and after the next consecutive loss the bet will be increased to 23 (22 plus 1). Starting with a bet of 5 units, this results in the following loss sequence:

| 5 | 11 | 23 | 47 | 95 | 191 | 383 | 767 |

before reaching a table limit of 1000 units.

The advantage to this variation is that whenever a series of losses is broken by a win, the net gain is greater than just the initial bet. Using the above sequence, a win after a string of four losses would result in a net gain of 9 units instead of 5 units for the standard Martingale system. This is calculated by subtracting the four losses, 5 + 11 + 23 + 47 = 86, from the 95-unit win for a net gain of 9 units. The net gain is always the initial bet plus one unit for each loss in a given sequence. In the standard Martingale, no matter how short or long the string of losses, the net gain after a win is always just the initial bet, in this case 5 units.

Some gamblers have concluded that if they doubled their bet and added two units instead of one after each loss, they could still sustain eight losses before running into the table limit. For those who have a lot of disposable funds, this line of thinking does have merit. If someone is going to take big risks, they may as well try to make it more worthwhile.

Reverse Martingale

Some gamblers feel confident enough not to chase their losses, as is done in the standard Martingale, but would rather take advantage of winning streaks. Instead of doubling the bet after every loss, in the reverse Martingale the bet is doubled after every win and reverts to the initial bet after every loss. As one can imagine, this system gets kind of tricky.

As with most "reverse" systems, good judgement has to be used in determining how far to carry a winning streak. One cannot just let it run to the table limit because a streak of eight consecutive wins occurs only about every 395 spins. Since the first loss will wipe out all potential gains from the streak, it has to be cut short (reverting to the initial bet) to preserve any profits. Since each spin of the ball is an independent event, how does one determine when a winning streak should be deliberately abandoned? That is the tricky part.

The D'alembert System

The D'Alembert system, also called *montant et demontant* (upwards and downwards), is often called a *pyramid* system. It was named after a French mathematician because it was based on a mathematical equilibrium theory he published more than 200 years ago. Since winning or losing large amounts using the D'Alembert system is unlikely, it is favored by players who want to keep the amount of their bets and losses to a minimum.

Like the Martingale, this system is mainly applied to the even-money outside bets. The betting progression is very simple: After each loss, one unit is added to the next bet, and after each win, one unit is deducted from the next bet. Starting with an initial bet of 5 units, a typical series would be as follows:

BET#	UNITS BET	RESULT	NET GAIN
1	5	lose	-5
2	6	win	+1
3	5	lose	-4
4	6	win	+2
5	5	win	+7
6	4	lose	+3
7	5	lose	-2
8	6	win	+4
9	5	lose	-1
10	6	lose	-7
11	7	win	0
12	6	win	+6

A series with long winning and losing streaks:

BET #	UNITS BET	RESULT	NET GAIN
1	5	lose	-5
2	6	lose	-11
3	7	win	-4
4	6	win	+2
5	5	win	+7
6	4	win	+11
7	3	win	+14
8	2	lose	+12
9	3	lose	+9
10	4	lose	+5
11	5	lose	0
12	6	win	+6

Exceeding the table limit is rarely a problem, but with a low initial bet, a string of wins (as in the above series) runs the risk of bumping into the table minimum, thereby breaking the sequence. This can be avoided by starting with a higher initial bet such as in the following example:

BET #	UNITS BET	RESULT	NET GAIN
1	10	win	+10
2	9	win	+19
3	8	lose	+11
4	9	lose	+2
5	10	lose	-8
6	11	win	+3
7	10	lose	-7
8	11	win	+4
9	10	win	+14
10	9	lose	+5
11	10	lose	-5
12	11	win	+6

In each of the above three samples, the player won six times and lost six times, resulting in a net gain of six units. The three sixes in the previous sentence are not a coincidence: *Whenever the number of wins equals the number of losses, the net gain is equal to the number of wins.* This is the beauty and elegance of the D'Alembert system that makes it a classic.

To use a more aggressive approach, increase the bet variation to two units, which results in double the net gain:

BET #	UNITS BET	RESULT	NET GAIN
1	10	win	+10
2	8	win	+18
3	6	lose	+12
4	8	lose	+4
5	10	lose	-6
6	12	win	+6
7	10	lose	-4
8	12	win	+8
9	10	win	+18
10	8	lose	+10
11	10	lose	0
12	12	win	+12

The fly in the ointment is that, over time, the number of wins is usually less than the number of losses for even-money bets. In fact, because of the zero and double-zero, on an American wheel an average of 18 wins and 20 losses will occur for every 38 spins of the ball. However, the system works fairly well on a single-zero wheel with the *le partage* or *en prison* rule, and this accounts for the popularity of the D'Alembert system in Europe.

Reverse D'Alembert

The reverse version of the D'Alembert system is sometimes called contra-Alembert. Like all "reverse" versions, it was probably devised by players who couldn't consistently win with the regular version. Using somewhat faulty logic, they decided that reversing the system rules would put them in the position of the casino, instead of the player. One of the earliest references to the reverse D'Alembert was by a Lord Beresford (whoever he was) in a pamphlet he published in 1926. It is doubtful, however, that he was the actual originator of the system.

The playing rules for the reverse version should be fairly evident: Decrease the bet by one unit after every loss and increase the bet by one unit after every win. As in the reverse Martingale, instead of chasing losses, this method builds on winning streaks and has the same problem of how to determine when a winning streak should be abandoned.

A common way of dealing with winning streaks is to revert to the initial bet after a predetermined number of consecutive wins. A typical number is four wins. The reverse D'Alembert system is surprisingly popular, an indication that it must be working for some people.

The Laboucher System

Another popular system is the Labouchere, also known as a cancellation system. Like the Martingale, it is a progressive method of betting, but is less likely to run up against the table limit. Although it is a French name, a connection has been made to a finance minister in the service of Queen Victoria, whose name was Labouchere and who had a taste for gambling. Whether or not he had anything to do with inventing the system is not certain.

The Labouchere system is more complicated than most, requires the use of a pencil and paper, and is applied only to the even-money outside bets. It starts with an arbitrary line of numbers such as 1-1-2-3. The initial bet is the sum of the first and last numbers in the line, in this case: 4. If the initial bet wins, the first and last numbers in the line are canceled, leaving: 1-2. The second bet would then be 3, the sum of the first and last numbers in the remaining line. If the second bet also wins, then the line is cleared and a new 1-1-2-3 line is started. Whenever the line is cleared, the net gain is the sum of the digits in the original line, in this case: 7.

Starting over with the original line, if the initial bet of 4 units loses, the amount of the bet is added to the end of the line. The new line is then: 1-1-2-3-4, and the next bet would be 5 (1 + 4). If the second bet also lost, it would again be added to the end and the line would become: 1-1-2-3-4-5. The following is a typical sequence:

BET LINE	BET	RESULT	NET GAIN
1-1-2-3	4	lost	-4
1-1-2-3-4	5	lost	-9
1-1-2-3-4-5	6	lost	-15
1-1-2-3-4-5-6	7	won	-8
1-2-3-4-5	6	won	-2
2-3-4	6	lost	-8
2-3-4-6	8	lost	-16
2-3-4-6-8	10	won	-6
3-4-6	9	won	+3
4	4	lost	-1
4-4	8	won	+7

The last win cleared the line with a net gain of 7 units, which is the sum of the numbers in the original line. The important point here is that a net gain was obtained with six losses and only five wins—a distinct advantage over the D'Alembert system.

It should also be noted in the above series that when the line got down to a single 4, the next bet was also 4. The rule is: When the line is reduced to a single number, that number is considered the total of the first and last numbers.

The starting line can be any length and contain numbers of any values or can be as simple as 1. The larger the numbers and the longer the line, the more aggressive the play. Other than the higher net gain, long lines do not seem to carry any special advantage; they just take more time to play out.

A short line with high numbers will increase the net gain but will also increase the betting levels and the capital required. Typical starting lines, from very mild to very aggressive, are:

Mild	1-1
	1-2
	1-1-1
	1-2-2
Aggressive	1-2-3-4

Although a betting line can be abandoned at any time, the potential net gain can only be assured if the line is played out. Since a loss adds one number and a win cancels two numbers, this will happen eventually. Of course, long strings of losses can drive the betting levels higher and higher, but the risk of running into the table limit is fairly low except with the more aggressive starting lines.

Reverse Labouchere

Although there is a tendency to belittle reverse versions of roulette betting systems, in 1966, an Englishman and his team of twelve players broke the bank at one of the French casinos in Nice with the reverse Labouchere system. The Englishman's name is Norman Leigh and some people have called him a con artist and accused him of exaggeration. That may or may not be true, but he did write a very interesting book about the experience.

As in the regular Labouchere system, a line of numbers is written down, and the first bet is the sum of the first and last numbers in the line. At this point the rules are reversed: Whenever a win occurs, the amount of the bet is added to the end of the line, and whenever a loss occurs, the first and last numbers in the line are canceled. When the line ultimately clears, there is a net loss instead of a net gain.

When Mr. Leigh and his team were playing, they used the aggressive starting line of 1-2-3-4, and every time the line played out it cost them ten units. Winning streaks were allowed to run to the table limit, if possible. The theory was that the small losses are eventually paid back when a long winning streak occurs. In the case of Norman Leigh and his companions it worked out as planned, but that does not mean it always will.

Inside Bet System

Inside bets are any bets placed directly on the main field of numbers. This includes single-number bets that pay 35:1 through six-number bets that pay 5:1, and everything in-between. It does not include dozens, column bets, or any even-money bets.

Most inside bet systems are based on the notion that a *sleeper* will eventually have to awaken. Although the term sleeper is the common vernacular, we prefer to use the more descriptive term: overdue number. It is commonly believed that if a particular number has not won in a long time, it is "due" or "overdue."

On the surface, the idea seems to have some merit. Since the probability of a given number winning is 1/38, or 1 chance out of 38, the expectation is that each number on the wheel will win an average of once every 38 spins of the ball. If a particular number has not appeared in, say, 70 or 80 spins, it is overdue and should show up very soon, if only to comply with the law of averages. What isn't always understood is that the so-called "law of averages" can only be relied on over a very long term. In roulette, a *long term* could mean thousands or tens of thousands of spins.

Actually, if a particular number comes up very seldom or not at all, it is probably because the wheel is not random. It is not at all difficult to cause a wheel, either accidentally or deliberately, to favor or disfavor certain numbers. If, for instance, the number 29 has not won in a long time, it may be because the pad at the bottom of the pocket had at one time been replaced during routine maintenance. If the replacement material had a different resilience, the ball may now bounce out of that pocket more readily than the other pockets. This would be enough to cause a substantial reduction in the probability of occurrence for number 29. Thus, any bet placed on that number is a losing proposition, even though the number always seems overdue.

Another point to remember is that a roulette wheel has no memory. Every spin of the ball is an independent event that has no bearing on what happened in the past. If the wheel is truly random, then the probability of a given number coming up continues to be 1 out of 38, no matter how long it has been since the last time that number won. Let us say the number 29 came up five times in the last 38 spins—five times the expectation. What is the probability of 29 winning on the 39th spin? If the wheel is unbiased: Exactly one chance out of 38.

Well, what happened to the law of averages? Was it repealed? Of course not. Three weeks later, on that same hypothetical wheel, number 29 may not show up for 200 spins of the ball. After the first 100 spins, some players will notice the "sleeper" and start betting on 29. One-hundred spins later, after they all lost their bankrolls, 29 finally appears. They do not believe it, but the law of averages is intact.

Any inside bet system that is based on the notion of overdue numbers should be avoided. The next chapter will describe a methodical way to play the inside numbers without depending on the arrival of an overdue number.

PLAYING THE SYSTEMS FOR PROFIT

The successful systems player rarely executes a classical roulette system in the manner in which it is described in the books. All systems have limitations and potential pitfalls that have to be mitigated. To be a consistent winner, therefore, requires adjustments in playing technique to overcome the weaknesses. These adjustments constitute the fine points of system play that will be described in this chapter.

Most mathematical betting systems are designed to work with even-money bets, which are the six bets along the outside of the roulette betting layout. They are: red, black, even, odd, low (1-18), and high (19-36). On a random wheel, these bets are all monetarily and statistically equivalent.

A Playable Martingale
As we saw in the previous chapter, the Martingale is a mathematically sound system, but the classical version has two problems that make it dangerous to play. The first is the limited number of loss doublings, sometimes only seven or eight, before the required bet gets so large that it runs into the table limit. The second, is the sizable bankroll that is at risk every time a sequential string of losses occurs.

Both problems can be mitigated with the proper application of *illusionary bets*. What in the world is an illusionary bet? It is a zero-value bet; a bet that is never actually placed and could also be called a *null* bet because no money is at risk.

When sitting at a table to play a Martingale, assuming a 5-unit minimum and 1000-unit maximum, the following loss string can be anticipated:

5	10	20	40	80	160	320	640

before reaching the table limit. If the eighth bet loses, we are in trouble, and as we saw in the last chapter, that can occur an average of every 170 spins of the ball. We will now look at a way to deal with this problem.

When first seated at the table, there are six even-money bets to choose from, and at least three of them just lost at the previous spin. If a bet is placed on one of the previous losers, that would effectively be the second bet in a potential loss string. The first bet was an illusionary bet. Because no money was at risk, we will call it a *null* bet. This null bet had the effect of extending the theoretical loss string to nine bets, one longer than before:

0	5	10	20	40	80	160	320	640

A string of nine successive losses will occur an average of every 323 spins—a big improvement.

This idea can be taken further by not placing the first bet until one of the even-money bets experiences two or three straight losses. To see the effect, assume that the first bet is not placed until three consecutive losses have occurred. The theoretical loss string will now start with three null bets and look like:

0	0	0	5	10	20	40	80	160	320	640

The table limit will not be encountered until the eleventh loss and this will occur on the average of every 1165 spins, the equivalent of twelve to fourteen hours of play.

A dilemma with trying to apply null bets while taking up a seat at a roulette table, is that a seated player is expected to place real bets for every spin of the ball. Ways to overcome this problem will be explained later in this chapter.

Another bet modification that some players apply is the CYA bet. A CYA bet is one that just covers previous losses without any opportunity of making a profit. After a few consecutive losses, recouping takes on more importance than making a measly 5-unit profit, and a CYA bet makes more sense than a doubling bet. Disregarding any null bets, observe the following example:

Standard doubling	5	10	20	40	Potential loss:	80
CYA at second bet	5	**5**	10	20	Potential loss:	40
CYA at third bet	5	10	**15**	30	Potential loss:	60

When playing the Martingale, the profits should be made on wins and after loss strings of no more than three spins in length. At the fourth or fifth successive loss, the goal should be to recoup the losses rather than to make a profit. Doing this will also gain an extra spin before encountering the table limit. With three null bets and a CYA bet after the fourth loss, the 1000-unit table limit will not be reached until the twelfth loss, as illustrated below:

Bet number:	1	2	3	4	5	6	7	8	9	10	11	12
Bet amount:	0	0	0	5	5	10	20	40	80	160	320	640

The expected probability of twelve losses in a row is 1/2213, or once every 2213 spins of the ball. This is a comfortable margin for most players. Of course, it *could* happen on the very next twelve spins, but it would not be much fun if there wasn't *some* risk.

In many casinos, a recent trend of dramatically increasing the maximum outside bet limits to $10,000 and higher has been observed. With three null bets and a CYA bet, this would allow as many as sixteen loss doublings. Sixteen straight losses has a probability of occurrence of 1/28844, or once every 28,844 spins of the ball. Again, it could happen on the very next sixteen spins, but it is more likely that your bankroll will run out long before.

Grand And Reverse Martingale

The grand and reverse versions of the Martingale are not recommended for ordinary players. The bankroll requirements can get very steep and we know of no certain way to mitigate the high risk levels for either version.

The D'Alembert System

The attractiveness of the D'Alembert system is that the bankroll requirement usually stays within reason. Unlike the Martingale, there is almost no risk of ever bumping into the table limit. The problem with it is that to clear the betting line takes the same number of wins as losses. As we know by now, for every 38 spins of the ball, the probability is that there will be 20 losses and only 18 wins.

The only way to overcome this obstacle is to start each sequence with null bets, such as described for the Martingale. The D'Alembert does not fare well when played on a double-zero wheel and is, therefore, not recommended for play in the United States. On a French wheel with the *en prison* rule, however, it gives good results for players that apply null bets and use sound judgement as to when to abandon a betting sequence and start over.

Reverse D'Alembert

Although, compared to the reverse Martingale, losses are likely to remain reasonable, we know of no sure way to overcome the inherent risks or how to insure good judgement in deciding when to abandon a winning streak. Therefore, this system is not recommended for ordinary players.

The Labouchere System

It seems surprising that the Labouchere system is not as popular as either the Martingale or the D'Alembert. It is based on the solid principle of canceling two losses with every win. Furthermore, running into the table limit is not very likely. Of course, if losses exceed wins by more than 2:1, then the player is in trouble, but this would be true no matter what system was being used.

Where most Labouchere players get into difficulty, is using too long and aggressive a starting line. This can lead to the kind of problem that depletes a bankroll rather quickly. A long starting line of 1-2-3-4-5-2-1 is tempting because clearing it results in a net gain of 18 units. Following is a short example of what can happen:

BET LINE	BET	RESULT	NET GAIN
1-2-3-4-5-2-1	2	won	+2
2-3-4-5-2	4	won	+6
3-4-5	8	lost	-2
3-4-5-8	11	lost	-13
3-4-5-8-11	14	won	+1
4-5-8	12	lost	-11
4-5-8-12	16	lost	-27
4-5-8-12-16	20	won	-7

After only eight spins, the bets are rapidly escalating and we are losing money even though, so far, we have the same number of wins as losses. Isn't one win supposed to cancel two losses? Yes, but it takes four wins just to cancel that long original starting line, even if no losses have occurred. That is the part of the Labouchere theory that is rarely mentioned and that most unsuccessful Labouchere players do not understand. In the above example, two of the wins canceled all four losses and the other two wins reduced the length of the bet line, but it will take two more wins to completely clear the line.

Although this is only one example, because of the additional wins needed to clear them, it should now be apparent that long starting lines are not at all advantageous. This is especially true since the full profit potential cannot be achieved until the line is completely cleared. In fact, a good rule to follow is: *The betting line should always be cleared as soon as possible.* Obviously, this cannot happen as readily with a long line as with a short line.

Consequently, Labouchere starting lines should be kept short to reduce the number of extra wins needed to clear the line. Recommended starting lines are: 1-1 or 1-2. Two-number starting lines need only one extra win to clear. The sequence 1-2-3-4 is a popular starting line whenever a minimum bet of 5 units is required. Actually, a line of 2-3 would be much better. The fact that 1-2-3-4 is popular, shows that most players do not fully understand the underlying principles of the Labouchere method.

Even when everything is done right, there will still be situations that get a little uneasy. If, for instance, the line starts getting long or the bets start to escalate, there is nothing wrong with abandoning the line altogether. Using a little judgement, a point can usually be chosen where the loss is minimized. In the previous example, a good place to abandon would have been after the third win, resulting in a profit of one unit.

Although, when played properly, the Labouchere holds up quite well on its own, starting a betting line only after observing the occurrence of at least one loss is prudent. Since any one of the six even-money bets can be chosen, this is just a matter of paying attention. Every system has its weaknesses, and the Labouchere is no exception. The ever-present danger is a series of short losing streaks (not uncommon) interspersed with only single wins.

A Modified Labouchere

As explained above, keeping the starting line short reduces the extra wins needed to clear the bet line. By carrying this a step further and eliminating the starting line altogether, no extra wins would be required. How can this be accomplished? Simple, just start the line with the first loss.

To do this, begin with an arbitrary bet, say, five units. If the bet wins, fine! That is a profit. If the bet loses, then the first number in the new line is a five and the following bet is five units. If it loses again, then the line becomes 5-5 and the next bet is ten units, as in the following example:

BET LINE	BET	RESULT	NET GAIN
none	5	lost	-5
5	5	lost	-10
5-5	10	lost	-20
5-5-10	15	lost	-35
5-5-10-15	20	won	-15
5-10	15	won	0
cleared			

It took only two wins to cancel four losses. No extra wins were needed to clear the line. At last we have arrived at what may be a pure version of the Labouchere, the only problem is that there wasn't any profit. But, that is easy to fix. All we have to do is add a one-unit kicker to each bet, and this will build up an accumulating profit.

BET LINE	BET	RESULT	NET GAIN
none	5	lost	-5
5	6	lost	-11
5-6	12	lost	-23
5-6-12	18	lost	-41
5-6-12-18	24	won	-17
6-12	19	won	+2
cleared			

Again, it took only two wins to cancel four losses and clear the line. The bets got a little higher, but we finished with a profit of two units, one for each win. If the kicker was two units, the profit would have been four units.

This is the most refined version of the Labouchere. Played properly, this system will hold up quite well unless the wheel runs more than 2:1 against the player. Another danger is the possibility of several short losing streaks separated by single wins. As in the regular Labouchere, if the line gets too long or the bets get too high, look for a good opportunity to abandon the line. And remember always to start a new bet series on an even-money bet that has just lost at least once or twice in succession.

Reverse LaBouchere

Despite the fact that Mr. Norman Leigh broke the bank at a French casino in 1966 using the reverse LaBouchere system, this system is not recommended for ordinary players. The bankroll requirements can get very steep and we know of no certain way to mitigate the high risk levels.

Playing The Inside Numbers

Most inside number systems are based on the expectation that an overdue number is more likely to win than numbers that have been winning regularly. As explained in the last chapter, such a system does not take into account that a wheel could be biased, or if it is unbiased, that the probability of 1/38 does not change from spin to spin.

We will describe one method that stretches your bankroll about as far as it can go and has better coverage than just continuously betting one unit on the same number. It starts with a dozen bet (which is actually an outside bet) and progresses to six-number bets, four-number bets, two-number bets, and finally straight-up bets. The progression is as follows:

Bet #	Type of Bet	Pays	Amount of Bet	Net Loss	Net Win
1	doz	2	1	1	2
2	doz	2	1	2	1
3	six	5	1	3	3
4	six	5	1	4	2
5	six	5	1	5	1
6	four	8	1	6	3
7	four	8	1	7	2
8	four	8	1	8	1
9	two	17	1	9	9
10	two	17	1	10	8
11	two	17	1	11	7
12	two	17	1	12	6
13	two	17	1	13	5
14	two	17	1	14	4
15	two	17	1	15	3
16	two	17	1	16	2
17	two	17	1	17	1
18	one	35	1	18	18
19	one	35	1	19	17
20	one	35	1	20	16
21	one	35	1	21	15
.	.	.	.	.	.
.	.	.	.	.	.
.	.	.	.	.	.
32	one	35	1	32	4
33	one	35	1	33	3
34	one	35	1	34	2
35	one	35	1	35	1
36	one	70	2	37	35
37	one	70	2	39	33
38	one	70	2	41	31
39	one	70	2	43	29
40	one	70	2	45	27

And so forth

To apply this sequence, the six-number bet should fall within the span of the original dozen. The four-number bet should then fall within the six, the two should be within the four, and the single number should be one of the two. In that way, the single number (Bet No. 18, onward) is included from the very beginning. If one chooses a particular number, but it does not come up soon, this would be a way to increase the chances of winning *something* during the first 17 spins. When the first win finally occurs, the sequence should be restarted from the beginning.

The only real advantage to the above sequence is that it is methodical. When it eventually wins, the result will always show a profit although it may be as small as one unit. Note that after every 35 spins, the bet must be doubled. The sequence can be modified by deleting lines that pay only one or two units, but then the jump to a two-unit bet will arrive sooner. No matter what is done, however, the overall odds do not change.

Playing the Systems

Anyone taking up a seat at a roulette table is expected to place minimum bets for every spin of the ball. This can be a problem when trying to use the null-bet gambit recommended above for the even-money betting systems. One way to get around this is to stand up and use casino chips instead of no-value roulette chips, but playing a system this way is difficult and tiresome.

A better way to deal with this is to play the system on two or three different even-money bets at the same time. When a line clears on one of the sequences, the others will still be going and, thereby, continue to meet the minimum bet requirement. Another way to deal with the minimum bet requirement is by placing a small bet on an inside number or by starting an inside number sequence as described above.

When playing an even-money system, always keep in mind that six different even-money bets are available on the roulette betting layout. If the wheel is unbiased, it does not matter which one is played—statistically they are all identical. Always watch all six to keep track of what null bets (losses) have already occurred. Then, when the current bet line is cleared, the outside bet on which to start the new line has already been scoped.

Don't ever forget that whenever a betting line is cleared, a different outside bet must be selected when starting the new line. At least switch to the opposite side. If, for instance, a line was just cleared on black, then red must have sustained at least one loss. Since every system eventually breaks down, never forget the cardinal rule of gambling: QUIT WHEN YOU ARE AHEAD!

A Final Word about System Play

System play is a more cerebral and methodical form of gambling that many seat-of-the-pants gamblers do not appreciate. Maybe they tried a system once and lost money because they did not know how to compensate for its weaknesses. As a result, many of them tend to denigrate all mathematical betting systems.

A similar situation exists in books on statistics. Yes, a case can be made to show that, in the long run, it is impossible to make a profit by playing the classical systems. None of these books, however, take into account any of the adjustments and modifications for mitigating system weaknesses that are outlined in this chapter. This may be because very little of this material has ever before been published.

Another reason could be that the statistical calculations get very complex when trying to generalize null bets and CYA bets. And statisticians have their way of rationalizing the possible paradox between the decreasing probability of the occurrence of winning/losing streaks as they get longer and the fact that each spin of the roulette ball is an independent event.

In Europe, where roulette players have the advantage of playing against a 1.35 percent house edge, system betting is very popular. Undoubtedly, many of these players have figured out how to mitigate the system limitations, and may even be using techniques that we don't know about. These are the players that grind out a small but steady return, while the flashy big-money players give the casinos their profits.

In the United States, where we have to deal with a much larger house advantage, making a consistent profit with system play is not as simple. However, if the techniques described in this chapter are applied intelligently and methodically, it should be easy enough to break even most of the time and occasionally make a small profit at minimal risk.

OLD TRICKS:
Gaffed Wheels

Roulette is a very old game, and clever people have been attempting to beat the odds for a long time. Up until the rapid expansion of Reno and Las Vegas after World War II, such attempts were sporadic and relatively few were successful. Casino growth in Nevada resulted in employment of large numbers of dealers and other casino personnel, many of whom became very familiar with the equipment and casino procedures. Using this knowledge base, some of them devised methods for beating the casino at various games, including roulette.

Long before players figured out how to cheat the casinos, however, the casinos were cheating the players. Before the state of Nevada legalized gambling in 1931, an honest roulette wheel was considered a rarity in the United States. The use of gaffed wheels was so standardized that they continued to be used in Nevada, even after gambling was legalized. It was not until the formation of the Gaming Control Board in 1955 that things began to change. And it was the Gaming Control Act of 1959, which instituted the Nevada Gaming Commission, that put real teeth into the law. After a while, most of the legal casinos in Nevada realized that they did not need dishonest wheels to make money, and decided that the risk of losing their gaming license was not worth the extra revenue.

The Nevada Gaming Control Board uses a technique called the *pickup* to catch cheating casinos. Gaming Control agents may walk into a casino at any time and randomly confiscate gaming equipment, which is then brought back to their laboratories and given a thorough inspection. This is the kind of procedure required to keep the casinos honest, and the reason that gaffed roulette wheels are no longer found in Nevada or, for that matter, in Atlantic City.

Because of the lack of gaming control board inspections, it is a given that almost all wheels in illegal gambling halls are dishonest. Be suspicious of roulette wheels in states other than Nevada and New Jersey, even if they are in legal establishments, because no other states have effective gaming control inspections. Even in other countries where gambling is legal, if the gaming inspection procedures are weak or the inspectors are easily bribed, the roulette wheels are probably dishonest.

Although verifying such statistics is impossible, it has been estimated that more gaffed wheels are sold than honest ones. In any case, a variety of interesting methods have been and still are being used to rig roulette wheels. In this chapter, we will describe the most interesting and the most common ways that dishonest gaming establishments use to gaff their wheels.

Ball Tripping

The preferred method for gaffing or rigging a roulette wheel, is to control into which pockets the ball will likely land. The best way to achieve this is by a procedure called *ball tripping*. Ball tripping is simply a means for prematurely dislodging the ball from the ball track so that it falls into a certain desired section of the wheelhead. It can be accomplished in a number of ways and has been regularly implemented in the past by both the casinos and the players.

Today, most casinos have installed plastic security shields around their roulette wheels, which effectively halted all ball tripping techniques used by players. Most illegal casinos and many casinos outside of Nevada and New Jersey, however, continue to employ ball tripping methods in their gaffed wheels. These methods take on the various forms that are described here.

Mechanical Wheel Gaffing

In one of the most common wheel gaffs, the dealer can control a trip pin that is located in the ball track. Whenever the dealer wants to kick the ball off the track, she moves a lever under the edge of the table. The lever is attached to a cable which is connected to a spring-loaded pin, causing it to project slightly into the ball track. As the ball comes around the track, it is tripped by the pin and falls into the wheelhead.

Most of the time, the dealer aims for 0 or 00 unless a heavy bet was placed on one of those numbers or someone is betting the center column. Dealers with visual tracking ability try to place the ball into a lightly-bet section of the wheelhead. Some dealers have gotten quite adept at this, leading people to believe that they are able to "aim" the ball when they spin it. Without the aid of the trip pin, however, there is no way the dealer can place the ball where she wants it.

Some of these wheels are equipped with a dealer-operated brake that can slow the wheelhead rotation. With this accessory, a skilled dealer can synchronize the wheelhead to the ball rotation so that when the ball encounters the trip pin, the wheelhead is in the correct position.

Although it would seem to be noticeable, a well-made trip pin is hard to detect. The pin is usually on the side of the wheel nearest the layout so that it can't readily be seen by the players. The hole in the track wall is very tiny and the pin is finer than a #6 sewing needle. See Figure 13-1. The ball track itself is partially recessed under the rim, so it is hard to get a good view of it without sticking one's head into the bowl.

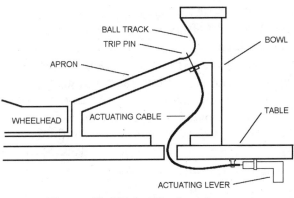

*Figure 13-1 Trip Pin Arrangement
in Gaffed Wheel*

In a more complex scheme, the wheel is gaffed with small blocking pins, one at the front wall of each ball pocket. Two hidden levers are located under the table at the dealer's side of the wheel. One lever actuates the pins in the red pockets and the other lever controls the pins in the black pockets. When one of the levers is moved, the pins are extended and the ball cannot enter that set of pockets. Since the pins protrude only when the wheelhead is turning, they are hard to see.

Because the blocking pins are in the wheelhead, the activating mechanism is more complicated than a trip pin and subject to occasional jamming. Although this gaff could block individual numbers of a particular color, it is primarily used against red/black bettors and, as such, is not a very elegant scheme.

A similar contrivance is called the *set wheel*. This is a wheel that can be set to favor one group of pockets by narrowing or widening the space between the frets, thus making one set of pockets wider and another set narrower. The wheel is gaffed so that alternate frets are attached to the center hub. When the hub is turned either way, the width of alternate pockets can be controlled. This gaff has an effect very similar to that of blocking pins, and is even less elegant.

Magnetic Wheel Gaffing

One of the simplest schemes using magnetics involves the replacing of some of the brass frets, which are non-magnetic, with frets made of steel, which is a magnetic material. The steel frets are carefully made to look identical to the brass ones. When a ball with a magnetic center is put into play, it is attracted to the steel frets and favors those pockets. Since the frets are permanently installed, the favored pockets have to be determined in advance. Most of the time the 0 and 00 are the chosen numbers. The dealer then controls whether to favor those pockets by switching the magnetic ball into or out of the game.

Prior to the takeover by Castro in 1959, gambling thrived in Cuba, and experienced gamblers knew that all the roulette wheels in Havana casinos were gaffed. Many gamblers took advantage of this by placing bets opposite to those of most of the players, because the ball usually fell into lightly-bet sectors of the wheelhead.

A standard way of fixing Cuban roulette wheels was with the use of electromagnets behind the ball track. The most common configuration consisted of four electromagnets equally-spaced inside the woodwork around the back side of the ball track as shown in Figure 13-2. The balls contained a steel core so they would react to the magnetic field. By pushing a button, the dealer could activate the electromagnets and kick the ball off the track at any of the four locations. Having four points on the track to choose from, placing the ball into the desired area of the wheelhead was relatively easy for a competent dealer.

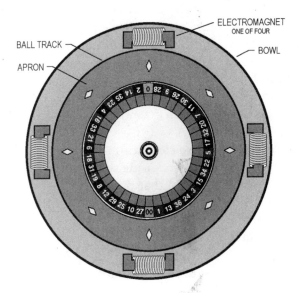

Figure 13-2 Location of
Electromagnets Inside Gaffed Wheel

Although many other magnetic gaffing schemes have been tried, none have been as successful as the Cuban method. An attempt to mount electromagnets in the wheelhead under selected number pockets turned out to be a maintenance headache. The main problem involved the transfer of electric current to the rotating wheelhead. This was done by means of several slip-ring contacts, one for each electromagnet plus a common return line. Even if this type of contact is regularly cleaned and adjusted, it is not very reliable. Furthermore, the frequent maintenance eventually betrays the fact that the wheel is gaffed to many more people than is desirable.

Modern Wheel Gaffing

Although the Cuban gaff is still in use today, modern technology has raised the sophistication of gaffed wheels to a new level. The main problem with most of the old methods is that wires or levers had to be run to and from the roulette wheel, which not only tied the wheel to the table, but made the gaffing more obvious. New methods have been invented in which the wires and mechanisms are hidden entirely within the wheel. External wires, buttons and levers are no longer in evidence.

One way to do this is to use electrically-operated blocking pins at each pocket. Behind each pin, inside the rotating wheelhead, is a miniature electrical solenoid that pushes the individual pin out whenever an electric current is applied. Each of the 38 solenoids is connected to an electronic circuit board containing a radio receiver and digital control circuits. The solenoids and the circuit board are powered by alkaline dry cells. The circuit board, the batteries, and all the wires are mounted under the cone of the wheelhead and rotate with it.

A remote control, similar to a small TV channel selector, is used to send a digitally-coded radio signal to the circuit board. This signal tells the digital circuits on the board to select one or more of the solenoid connections and apply the necessary activating current. The remote control, which is operated by someone other than the dealer, can be set in advance, before the spinning ball drops, to block the pockets of heavily-bet numbers. As the ball drops into the wheelhead, the activating button is pressed and blocking pins emerge for a few seconds, just long enough to prevent the ball from entering the designated pockets.

This is essentially a maintenance-free system that is totally hidden inside the wheelhead of the roulette wheel. Thus, the entire roulette wheel can be rotated, leveled, or moved about, just like an honest wheel, with no evidence that it is any different. The digital circuitry and miniature solenoids use so little power that the batteries last a long time, and are typically replaced only once a year.

Who is Cheating Whom?

As previously mentioned, any time you see roulette wheel action in any of the forty-eight states other than Nevada or New Jersey, assume the wheel is gaffed. You will be correct 90 percent of the time. Furthermore, some of the players will *know* the wheel is gaffed, but will continue betting anyway. This is the "only game in town" syndrome, which is a subject for another book.

By not recognizing the definition of the word *ethics*, the casinos have set themselves up to be fair game for any kind of scam. The use of gaffed wheels and other casino cheating devices provides justification for players to do the same. As a result, clever people have devised a variety of interesting ways to beat the odds. The most prevalent and most interesting of these will be described in the next chapter.

OLD TRICKS: Players' Revenge

Fifty years ago, casino pit bosses concentrated most of their surveillance on blackjack and craps, looking for card cheats and dice switchers. Roulette was virtually ignored because, apart from past posting, it was thought to be relatively cheat-proof. Besides, many wheels were gaffed by the casinos and they felt that they had complete control. In the days before plastic security screens were used, players would crowd around the wheel, leaning on it and even placing their hands on the outside rim. During off hours when the game was shut down, the roulette chips and the balls were removed or locked up, but the wheel itself was left open and unprotected. Today, when a wheel is not in use, it is secured with a locked cover. As we will see, there is good reason for this.

Past Posting

The term *past posting* originated in horse racing and simply referred to a bet placed on a winner after the race was over. Today, the application of past posting is most prevalent at roulette tables, although it is occasionally employed at other table games such as blackjack. American roulette is particularly vulnerable because, most of the time, only one dealer is present. Although the floor supervisor provides a second set of eyes, this person's attention can be diverted in many ways.

Past posting continues to be the most common form of player cheating at an American roulette table. The moment the ball settles into a numbered pocket, the dealer has to glance at the wheelhead to learn the winning number. A sharp-eyed player will also see it, and while the dealer's eyes are momentarily diverted from the layout there is an opportune moment to quickly move a palmed chip onto the winning number. Some players do not even bother palming a chip, but just slide a stack from a losing number to the winning number. An accomplished past poster can do this with a quick hand motion that is hardly noticed by the other players.

Past posting is frequently executed by a two-person team. The spotter sits or stands next to the wheel, watches where the ball drops, and signals the bettor. The bettor, who is sitting at the far end of the betting layout, has previously placed a stack of chips on the center column. Upon getting the signal, the bettor then quickly slides the stack to the left or to the right, or leaves it alone if the center column is the winning bet. Done expertly, this is very difficult to spot.

A move that is also difficult to spot is done by a bettor who is holding chips in her fingers while concealing other chips in the palm of her hand. The bettor starts to place a late bet but withdraws her hand without depositing the chips held by her fingers. This action looks innocuous to most observers, because they have no idea that palmed chips were dropped on the winning number.

Sometimes a team will set up a more complicated scam in which the dealer is distracted by one player while another player slips money chips under the win marker. The variations of past posting are almost endless and this is one reason that controlling it is difficult.

Casinos train their dealers to be constantly on the alert for practitioners of the art. Usually, the first time the dealer sees it happen, she will simply disallow the bet. If it happens a second time, she will alert the floor supervisor. After that, the supervisor's eyes, as well as the security camera, will be watching the layout, and the scam is over. If the casino has a video tape that shows that the past posting was deliberate, they will not hesitate to prosecute.

Bouncing Pads

It was a year or so after the *superball* hit the market when Clark got the idea. The superball was a toy ball, made out of a very resilient rubber compound so that it could bounce really high. Clark was an acquaintance of mine who, in times past, had worked as a casino dealer and pit boss, and beating roulette was an obsession of his.

Being a very clever person, the extreme resiliency of the superball gave Clark an interesting notion. What if a thin piece of superball material were placed in the bottom of a roulette wheel pocket? Any ball entering that pocket would bounce out and that number would rarely be a winner. He first attempted to make thin sheets of material by slicing a superball with a razor, but the results were always crude and irregular. After doing a little legwork, he located the material supplier and found that the same resilient rubber was available in thin sheets. Of course, he bought some right away and started experimenting at home on his own roulette wheel.

Clark could not believe how well it worked: The ball simply would not stay in any pocket that had a superball pad. Moreover, the material was black, so when it was placed in the bottoms of the black pockets, it was almost invisible. Now, he just had to figure out how to get the material installed in a casino wheel. He realized it would take inside help in Las Vegas because the casinos are open twenty-four hours. However, Clark knew that in the Bahama Islands many casinos were only open in the afternoons and evenings.

A few weeks later, Clark and a partner flew to Nassau to reconnoiter the situation. The very next morning, while strolling around the hotel lobby, Clark wandered through a slightly-open door and found himself all alone in the casino gaming room. In those days, they did not open the tables until about four in the afternoon. Always prepared, he had the precut pads in his pocket, along with a small tube of cement. It only took him about three minutes to install eight or ten pads in a roulette wheel. He then wandered back out of the room before anyone saw him. His original plan was to put in two or three pads, but this turned out to be so easy that he got carried away.

When the casino opened at four, Clark and his partner were the first players betting at the rigged wheel. They laid their bets on red and won and won and won. Very soon, a crowd started to gather and more and more players were betting black, thinking that black was long overdue. They all lost. Clark now realized that he put in too many pads and wished that black would win at least once so that the fix was not so obvious. By now, all the pit supervisors were also watching the wheel, completely fascinated by this red, red, red phenomena.

After 22 reds in a row, Clark could tell that the pit supervisors were getting ready to shut down the wheel. Since they were about the only players betting on red, Clark and his companion decided to cash in and make themselves scarce. When someone eventually inspected the wheel and found those bouncy pads, the two of them would have been prime suspects.

The point to this story is that something as simple as resilient pocket pads can rig a roulette wheel in a major way. Today, the casinos in Nassau are open twenty-four hours a day, and any table that is closed has a locked cover over the wheel—just like in Las Vegas. Although this kind of fix is no longer as easy to accomplish, you can depend on the fact that many older roulette wheels out there do not have uniformly-resilient pads in all 38 pockets.

Wiggly Frets

When a roulette ball starts bouncing around inside the wheelhead, it usually strikes several pocket separators before settling into a pocket. These separators, or frets, are made out of brass or aluminum and are rigidly mounted in the wheelhead. When the ball strikes one of them, it rebounds strongly—like a billiard ball bouncing on a smooth concrete floor.

If a fret is loosened, it has the effect of absorbing the energy in the ball and arresting the bounce. In fact, a properly-loosened fret will usually cause the ball to land in an adjacent pocket. The only requirement for this to work, is that the ball has to eventually strike one of the loosened frets before it lands in a different pocket. Consequently, loose frets work best with lively balls that bounce around and contact most of the separators before settling into a pocket.

Although the separators can be loosened with a pair of pliers, the professional uses a small homemade tool with a slot that is just the thickness of the fret. The tool is slipped over the fret and twisted slightly, an action that takes just a moment to do—even quicker and easier than installing pocket pads. Again, this is one of those old fixes that was prevalent when roulette wheels were more readily accessible to outsiders.

Just as with the pocket pads, however, you can depend on the fact that many older roulette wheels out there do not have uniformly-rigid separators between all 38 pockets. When frets have been deliberately loosened, it was usually done at only two or three numbers so that the effect is subtle, but strong enough to win the money. Occasionally, the column two sector on an American wheel was fixed by loosening the frets from about pocket 35 through 17, while skipping 0, 7, 9, 28, and 30.

Manual Ball Tripping

Although visual tracking is not illegal, this technique was frequently applied in conjunction with actions considered illicit by casino personel. One of those actions was called *manual ball tripping*.

There were various forms of manual ball tripping, one was called the finger trip. It was a very brazen trick, in which a visual tracker would physically knock the ball off the track at the right moment. This scam took two people: a bettor and a tracker with a sharp eye, nerves of steel, and impeccable timing. The bettor, frequently a bubbly, outgoing woman sitting at the far end of the table, would make a bet on the center column or other combination covering a contiguous span of numbers in the wheelhead.

The tracker had to be standing right next to the wheel with one hand resting on the rim. During the last few revolutions of the ball, the tracker could visually determine when the ball was about to cross the chosen section of numbers at a point near his hand. When the bettor got a signal from the tracker, she would do something to attract attention, such as squealing with delight or knocking over a stack of chips. Just then, the tracker flicked a finger over the rim, knocking the ball off the track into the desired section of numbers. Done expertly, this is not as obvious as it seems.

For cheaters that felt the finger trip was a little too risky, the horsehair trip was made to order. This trick required a minor modification to the wheel that, in the old days of sloppy surveillance, was not that hard to accomplish. A horizontal hole had to be drilled between the back of the ball track and the outside of the bowl. While they were at it, they usually drilled four holes that were evenly spaced around the perimeter, so that no matter how the wheel was positioned, one of the holes was always accessible from the player's side of the table.

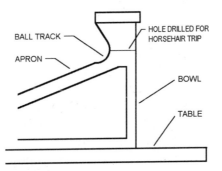

*Figure 14-1 Location of Hole Used
for Horsehair Ball Trip*

Having seen the holes, I haven't a clue where they got drills that small and that long. The holes were very tiny, even smaller than those used with the built-in trip pin device. They only had to be big enough to pass a horsehair, which was the tripping device of choice because it had just the right amount of stiffness. The horsehair trip was not only less obvious than the finger trip, but eliminated the need for distractions or precise signaling.

Ball tripping was an extremely common scam practiced by both the house and the players. If you have access to some old or antique roulette wheels, an interesting exercise would be to examine the ball track under a bright light. Look very carefully and do not be surprised when you find ball-trip holes. Nowadays, however, the plastic shields that the casinos place around their roulette wheels prevent such shenanigans from occurring.

Magnetic Tripping

Another way of tripping the ball is with the use of an external electromagnet. This had the advantage of not requiring any prior wheel modifications, and in the days before magnetic detectors, was virtually undetectable. Today, activating a powerful electromagnet near a roulette wheel would almost certainly set off an alarm.

To use an electromagnet required the substitution of a special ball with a steel core. This was done either with the help of the dealer or by means of a sleight-of-hand trick. Just as a visual tracker could knock the ball off the track with the flick of a finger, in this case, instead of tripping the ball, it was scooped up with two fingers. At the same moment, a palmed steel-core ball was dropped into the wheel. Of course, these incidents occurred before the introduction of plastic security shields.

In the most customary application, a woman's handbag containing an electromagnet was placed right next to the wheel as shown in Figure 14-2. The handbag had to be large and sturdy to hold a bulky electromagnet and heavy batteries. The distance between the electromagnet and the ball track was typically three to four inches, which is a long reach for a magnetic field to be effective. This dictated the use of a high-current device that caused the batteries to wear out quickly.

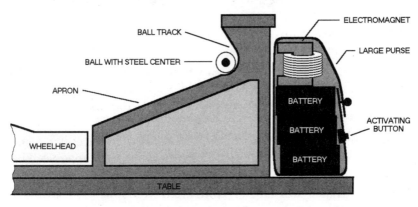

Figure 14-2 Electromagnet Hidden in Purse

Several methods were employed to overcome this problem, but one of the most unique made clever use of a wheelchair. Sometime in the 1960's, a woman in a self-propelled electric wheelchair was pushed up to a roulette wheel at a Las Vegas Strip casino. Although two heavy-duty automobile batteries were sitting on a shelf under the seat, it did not strike anybody that the wheelchair was being pushed and was not running on its own power.

The batteries, in fact, were connected to a powerful electromagnet in a large handbag on the woman's lap. As soon as the wheelchair was maneuvered into position, the woman hoisted her handbag onto the roulette table and plopped it right next to the wheel. At the time, it seemed like a natural thing to do and nobody paid much attention to her. The woman seemed to be mesmerized by the spinning wheel and then someone at the far end of the table started to win and win and win. At one point, the big winner cashed in and disappeared. About the same time, someone rolled away the woman in the wheelchair, and they also disappeared. This event was probably repeated any number of times at different casinos.

As cute as the wheelchair idea was, it was still a brute-force system. Eventually, this piqued the curiosity of technically-competent people. With their knowledge of magnetics and electronic circuit design, they designed elegant solutions to the problem.

One of these designs used a power thyristor as a switch to dump the stored electrical charge from a large capacitor through a toroid magnetizing coil. (A thyristor is an electronic switch used to control the flow of current; a toroid is a coil wound on a donut-shaped core that is designed to concentrate the magnetic field.)

Depending on the polarity of the current flow in the coil, it could either magnetize or demagnetize a strong permanent-magnet. This equipment was powered by ordinary alkaline dry cells and was so compact that it was entirely contained in a small box easily attached to the underside of a roulette table with double-faced tape. The magnet was then activated or deactivated at will with a simple remote-controlled device such as a garage-door opener. After the money was made, the equipment usually had to be abandoned, and was eventually found by the casino. It was this kind of clear and unambiguous evidence that finally convinced many casinos to install magnetic detection equipment.

What is Next?

So far in this book, we have described every conceivable way to beat a roulette wheel, except one. Much of this material has never been published before, anywhere. The people who use these methods tend to avoid publicity and are probably peeved that their techniques are being exposed at this time.

The remaining method is computer prediction, which is covered in the next two chapters. The information is presented for educational purposes to show that with sufficient ingenuity such a project can be accomplished. The information will also benefit the many casino operators who were unaware that computer prediction is alive and well. By now, it is probably being done in a more sophisticated and elegant way than our old-fashioned approach which was developed over ten years ago.

NEW TRICKS: Computer Prediction

The first digital computers were very large, cumbersome machines that used thousands of vacuum tubes, with antiquated input/output devices that were based on teletype equipment. In those days, the notion of ever using a computer to predict the outcome of a roulette game would have seemed ludicrous. Since the transistor had not yet been invented, it was hard to imagine the impact that solid-state electronics would have in the future of computers.

By the 1960s, however, transistors and integrated circuits were rapidly replacing the vacuum tubes, resulting in smaller, faster, and more powerful machines. Even when the development of the microprocessor made digital computers compact enough that they could be installed on an office desk, most of us could still not envision using one for roulette prediction. However, some people had more imagination. It was the early 1980s when I learned of a serious attempt to develop a roulette prediction program. My first thought was: "Even if suitable software could be written, where would the hardware be installed?" Even with inside help, this task would not be a simple matter.

Many casinos were now installing elaborate closed-circuit television security systems. This was made to order for surreptitiously locating computer equipment amongst the security electronics.

(To the untrained eye, one rack of electronic equipment looks the same as the next.) Since an overhead security camera was always pointed at each roulette table, it could be used for timing the ball and the wheelhead.

A person viewing the monitor in the security room would click on a switch to feed timing pulses into the computer. A moment later, the computer would spit out a prediction that would then be transmitted by radio to a person placing bets at the wheel. As awkward as this arrangement was, I had to admit that it was technically feasible. In the case I was familiar with, however, the project failed because the programmer could not make the software work consistently. That is not to say, that this was not done successfully somewhere else.

That programmer has my sympathy, because as I subsequently found out, the software solution can be a bit tricky and elusive. For most people, the correct approach is not immediately obvious.

The Wrong Way

Most programmers begin logically by working out the physics and motion dynamics to devise a mathematical model of a theoretically-perfect roulette wheel. The model requires some basic data such as the position, velocity, and deceleration of both the ball and the wheelhead at a given point in time. Although creating this model is not an easy task, it has to be done correctly. Whatever software prediction method is used, the proper mathematical relationship between the position of the ball and the position of the wheelhead at any time has to be known.

Some analysts, after having done a good job on the mathematical model, then make their first mistake. They write a roulette prediction program based solely on the model. Uh, uh, it ain't that easy. I ought to know; I wasted a lot of time fooling with such a program before I fully understood that real-world roulette wheels are not "theoretically perfect." Although this is a rather obvious fact, for some of us, it takes a long time to sink in.

The trouble with this blind alley is that it can take a long time to realize that the problem is conceptual. You stick with it because sometimes the program will seem to work, and sometimes it will not. You will think that it only works early in the day because that is when you are alert and your timing is more accurate (or vice-versa). You will think the timing loops in the program are not sufficiently accurate. You will think the mechanical timing switches are too sensitive, or not sensitive enough. You will think your mathematical model is flawed. You may even think there are intermittent bugs in the program. And on and on and on.

I spent six months trying to fix all the things I thought were going wrong. In fact, I would have given up the project as an impossible task except that I continued hearing that someone was out there beating the wheels with a computer. My ego told me, "If someone else can do it, then I can do it." It was a challenge from which I could not walk away.

One night, after an unsuccessful test at the old Nevada Club in Laughlin, my partner and I were commiserating at the Riverside Casino bar while watching the sun rise. Suddenly, it made sense. It was as though I had been stumbling around in a twilight zone, when a light was switched on. I instantly comprehended the problem and knew I had been doing it all wrong. Some people will probably see this almost immediately, while others will never see it. With me, it took half a year.

At the time, I was using a Sharp PC-1500 pocket computer with 16 kilobytes of RAM. In the early 1980's, this was the latest and greatest in commercial compact equipment. The Sharp had a built-in BASIC interpreter so that the entire 16K was available for actual code. The program I wrote was rigidly based on my mathematical model, and by writing efficient code, I could squeeze it into the available 16K. The predicted result was obtained from the computer by using the built-in BEEP statement. Long and short beeps were transmitted by radio to my partner, and he had to count them to know what numbers to bet on.

Earlier that evening at the Nevada Club, although the wheel we were working was heavily biased, no matter what we did, we could not make the program function. I even noticed that the ball drop always occurred in the same sector on the rim, so I went out to our car in the parking lot and rewrote the program. I hard-coded the drop sector into the program, thus eliminating one of the variables, but this still did not do any good. However, it did plant the germ of an idea into my head: "What if I could hard-code all of the specific characteristics of that particular wheel into the program?"

Later that night at the Riverside bar, that germ turned on a light in my brain that caused me to rethink the entire problem. I realized that the wheelhead deceleration for every roulette wheel is different, depending on the type and condition of the bearings, and when they were last lubricated. The same is true for the deceleration of the ball, which is dependent on the type and condition of the ball track, and to a lesser extent, the size and weight of the ball.

Then we have the problem of accurately predicting the ball drop point, which is absolutely necessary for a successful outcome. In the mathematical model, whenever the ball slows to a certain minimum velocity, it is presumed that it will drop off the track. For real roulette wheels, it does not always happen that way. When it reaches that minimum velocity, it may hang in for another half turn because the track is slightly warped. Or it may drop a half turn earlier because of a slight bump or wear groove in the track. In other words, no mathematical model can predict just when and where the ball will drop, and *accurately determining the drop point is absolutely critical for formulating a prediction.*

The Right Way
So, how do we overcome the deficiencies of the mathematical model? It is really very simple: When a particular wheel is selected for play, it must first be characterized so that its unique traits can be used as the database for the operating program.

Although the idea sounds simple enough, its implementation can get somewhat involved.

Before we continue, a brief explanation of a typical hardware setup would be instructive. The timing input device is a small manually-operated push-button switch, which is connected by means of a thin, flexible cable to a pocket-sized computer. The output signal from the computer is usually taken from its internal speaker line, and is fed into a miniature radio transmitter. The full details on these hardware configurations are covered in the next chapter.

To operate this setup takes a two-person team: a timing person and a bettor. The timing person clicks the push-button switch (hidden in a pocket) to enter timing pulses into the computer (hidden under her clothes). Using the timing information, the program calculates a prediction that is transmitted to the bettor, who is at the far end of the roulette table. The prediction, which the bettor hears in an earphone, may be a series of long and short beeps, or it may be a computer-synthesized voice. The bettor then quickly lays down bets based on the prediction. The lapsed time between the last timing click and the transmission of the computer's prediction to the bettor is less than one second.

Charecterizing the Wheel

Characterizing a roulette wheel is easily done with the aid of a rudimentary data collection program. Apart from containing a timing loop or a counter, this program does not perform any calculations, it simply collects and stores a time pulse whenever a push-button switch is clicked. The timing data can be stored in a program array or in a separate data file.

Collecting data that represents the wheelhead deceleration is a simple matter. The timing person, who is standing next to the wheel, just clicks the pocket switch once for every revolution of the wheelhead as it slowly decelerates. This is done by focusing on a fixed reference point on the far side of the apron and clicking every time the zero (or double-zero) passes that reference point.

See Figure 15-1. This timing data very neatly defines a deceleration curve for the wheelhead. It also provides the foundation for a database that, for any wheelhead velocity, will give its rotational position at any later point in time.

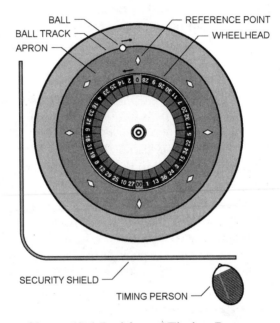

Figure 15-1 Position of Timing Person

Collecting data on the ball characteristics is a little more complicated. As with the wheelhead, the timing person clicks the switch every time the ball passes the fixed reference point. The last click is the exact moment when the ball drops off the track and falls into the wheelhead. This information is enough to generate a database that, for any ball velocity, will give the relative time to the drop point.

The timing person then has to record the drop point location. This is done by mentally dividing the track periphery into eight or sixteen sectors, using the ball deflectors (canoe stops) as delineators. The sectors should be mentally numbered from 1 to 8 or 1 to 16, starting from the reference point and counting clockwise. After the ball drops, the sector number is clicked into the computer. There is usually plenty of time to do this before the dealer spins the ball again. With this information added to the ball database, the wheel sector at any drop point will also be known.

Whether to use an eight-sector or a sixteen-sector system depends on the accuracy goal of the program. I even tried a 32-sector system, but all it did was complicate the data refinement process. Once the wheel characterization data has been collected, it must be evaluated, adjusted, refined, and reformatted for the operational program. This is done with the aid of two data processing programs, one for the wheelhead and one for the ball. At first, we had very rudimentary programs so that most of the data crunching had to be done manually. For a single wheel, it took us two to three hours to turn the raw characterization data into usable databases. Ultimately, when the processing programs were polished to where most of the data crunching was done automatically, the entire procedure took less than twenty minutes.

Playing the Wheel

The two databases can now be loaded into the operational play program, and the team is ready to go. When both team members are suitably positioned at the roulette table, the timing person begins the routine. When the ball has slowed to about six or seven revolutions from the drop point, she times the wheelhead by entering two successive clicks, one revolution apart. This is immediately followed by two more clicks, one revolution apart, for the ball. After receiving the fourth click, the computer automatically goes to work and calculates a prediction, which is immediately transmitted to the bettor.

Done correctly, the second timing click for the ball is entered about the fourth or fifth revolution before it drops off the track.

This allows just enough time for the bettor to hear the prediction and place bets on ten to twelve numbers. If the timing is done much earlier, the program accuracy falls off rapidly. We found that a betting spread of ten to twelve numbers is needed to cover typical ball bounce and timing inaccuracy.

The way the operational program works is that the first two clicks establish the wheelhead position and velocity at a known point in time. The second two clicks establish the ball position and velocity at a slightly later point in time. The program then looks up the ball velocity in the ball database for that wheel to learn its predicted drop-off time as well as the sector position from which it will leave the track. With the drop-off time identified, the program is able to consult the wheelhead database to obtain the wheelhead position at the time the ball drops. Knowing the ball position and the wheelhead position at the predicted drop-off time, the program now has enough information to determine what number will be beneath the ball when it falls into the wheelhead.

If you kept track, you would have figured out that this entire procedure involves the use of the following five programs:

1. Data collection for wheelhead
2. Data collection for ball
3. Data processing for wheelhead
4. Data processing for ball
5. Operational play

In actual practice, the two data collection programs should be combined so that all the data can be collected during a single trip into the casino. This requires the use of an audible menu (an on-screen menu would not be practical in the casino) to switch between the two functions. By now, it is probably also obvious that more than one pocket switch is needed. Details of these required items will be covered later.

Enhancing the Software

As mentioned above, the prediction can be transmitted to the bettor in two different ways. One is a series of beeps and the other is a voice synthesizer. Each method has its advantages.

Considering the broadness of the radio frequency spectrum, it is unlikely that anyone would intercept the transmitted radio signal, especially since the transmitter is very low power and very short range. On the small chance that someone does intercept the signal, however, hearing a synthesized voice reciting a series of numbers could raise an eyebrow, whereas a string of beeps would not get much attention. Another advantage of the beep system is that almost any kind of microwatt transmitter will work just fine.

With the voice synthesizer, however, a stable FM transmitter with a decent audio modulator is needed to avoid fading and to have good intelligibility. This is not a difficult thing to do, it just means that a lot more attention has to be devoted to the transmitter/receiver equipment.

The advantage to using the voice synthesizer is that the bettor does not have to count and interpret a series of beeps. Another advantage is that it allows use of a more elaborate audio menu system, which can increase the flexibility of the operation.

As we said earlier, the bettor gets the computer prediction by way of an earphone attached to a radio receiver. The timing person should also be wearing an earphone, which can be attached directly to the computer speaker line. The internal speaker itself should, of course, be disconnected. Providing an earphone for the timing person opens the door for additional software enhancements.

The Audio Menu

An audio menu system is an important adjunct for both the data collection and operational programs. The data processing programs can, of course, use a normal on-screen menu. An advantage of the voice synthesizer is that it can serve double-duty as a voice menu in the field. Although a menu system based on beeps can be devised, it will be more limited.

With the use of an audio menu, the two data collection programs can be combined and the timing person can switch between them at will. It can also facilitate collecting data from more than one wheel without having to leave the casino premises. Rather than waste idle time, it is a major advantage for the timing person to be able to move from wheel to wheel as conditions change.

The same advantages apply to the operational program. If several wheels have been characterized, the timing person can select any one of them and the team can move from wheel to wheel at will. One way to arrange this in the program is to maintain separate databank files for each wheel. When the timing person activates the menu and selects a particular wheel, the appropriate database files are loaded into the program, and it is ready to go. Even with a slow computer, this takes only a few seconds. If the team decides to switch wheels, the timing person uses the audio menu to select the new wheel. This causes the program to redimension the data arrays and load in the new files.

Real-Time Compensation

Once the programs are up and running reliably, additional enhancements can be added. These are limited only by the imagination and ingenuity of the programmer. One refinement that is worth mentioning is real-time compensation.

While the team is in the process of working a wheel, certain events can occur that affect the accuracy of the predictions. These can be as obvious as the dealer switching to a different size ball, or as subtle as fatigue causing a change in the timing person's reaction time. These are things that can produce a rotational shift in the number prediction. So long as the shift is consistent, the program can be made to compensate for it on a real-time basis.

To do this, the timing person needs to enter the actual winning number after the computer has made its prediction. The program compares the actual number with the predicted number, determines how far off the prediction was, and maintains a running average of the difference. If the running average is consistently in one direction, it begins to adjust the future predictions accordingly.

Since the timing person could easily lose count when clicking in a large number with a single switch, an entry system of tens and units should be devised. The 0 and 00 should be assigned specific numbers larger than 36 that the computer will recognize as such. Other special numbers can also be assigned for specific purposes, such as telling the computer to ignore a particular entry.

When the program makes its prediction, it does not consider ball bounce, but assumes that the ball drops directly into the wheelhead and stays in place. Since ball bounce is generally unpredictable, the selection of a wheel that exhibits minimal ball bounce is important. Sometimes, however, the bounce is consistent enough that the program can compensate for it.

To take full advantage of the compensation, requires good judgement and close observation by the timing person. If the bounce consistently occurs in one direction, then the timing person should enter the number that the ball finally settled in. The program will then compensate for the bounce. If the bounce seems random, then the timing person should enter the number of the pocket that the ball first landed in, prior to any bouncing.

Writing the Programs

Once the concept is understood, writing the necessary programs is not a particularly difficult task for an accomplished programmer. Not being certain about the legal implications, I decided not to provide any actual program code. Furthermore, every project is different, and so long as the correct approach is being used, starting from scratch is usually easier than trying to analyze and modify existing code. Besides, the programmer may prefer to use an entirely different programming language.

The first programs for this project were written for the BASIC interpreter built into the Sharp PC-1500 pocket computer. Later versions of the programs with a voice synthesizer output and voice menus were compiled in QuickBASIC. This should tell you that just about any programming language will work well. In actual operation, after the four timing clicks are entered, the results are spit out in a fraction of a second. Thus, calculation speed is not a problem and the use of assembly language or a math coprocessor need not even be considered. In fact, most of the processing time consists of database lookups.

We never took it this far, but a really adept programmer could fully-automate and integrate the data processing to eliminate the manual data-refining procedure. The program could then be written so that everything (data collection, processing, and playing) is done during a single trip into the casino. The timing person could walk in and start collecting characterization data, and the program would be processing it on a real-time basis. Every so often, the program could be tested to see if the predictions were accurate enough to start playing. The result would tell the timing person if more data should be collected or if it was time to signal the bettor to buy in and start laying down the bets.

We mentioned earlier that this project requires five programs. This is true, but having a sixth program specially-designed to remove some drudgery from the lab testing is very convenient. This should be a carbon copy of the operational play program except for a different output. The modified output should be designed so that each time the ball is spun, the predicted result is displayed on the screen and also added to a data file. The actual numbers, with *and* without ball bounce, should then be added to the data file by entering them on the keyboard. At a later time, this data file can be analyzed to see how accurate the predictions were. To provide more diagnostic information, the predicted and actual drop sectors can also be recorded.

THE EQUIPMENT

Once the software is developed to the point that computer prediction of roulette may be a viable project, the hardware phase
begins to take on more importance. It will then become apparent
that developing the hardware is not a trivial pursuit. While the
software can be created and tested in a laboratory setting using a
standard desktop computer, the actual application of that software in a field environment is a totally different situation.

The Eudaemonic Pie by Thomas Bass is a very interesting and educational book in that it provides a good lesson on how not to
design the field hardware. In the late 1970s, a team composed
mainly of Physics PhDs, designed and built a miniature computer
from scratch. Since commercial pocket-sized computers were not
yet available, they used an early microprocessor chip, an Intel
6502, and programmed it using machine language—a very difficult task.

Though they did an incredibly good job on the software, any competent electrical engineer could have told them that their hardware approach would lead to problems. They were so paranoid
about being caught that they embedded all the equipment (computer, radio transmitter, batteries) in the soles and heels of their
shoes. (Did they think that if they were strip-searched, no one
would examine their shoes?) As a result, they were plagued with
equipment failures, mainly due to broken wires and connectors.

When my partner and I started our project, custom designing a
portable computer was not necessary, since the Sharp PC-1500
was already on the market. Although, ultimately we found the
Sharp to be inadequate, it did carry us a long way. It got us through
all the blind alleys that finally led us to the correct software solution. It was only when we tried to make the software more sophis-

ticated that it faltered due to the awkwardness of the cassette-tape method for program storage and the limited memory.

By now, I had switched to QuickBASIC, which allowed me to compile the programs. I was also automating the data-refining procedure and adding the synthetic speech capability. To handle this, we needed a standard computer in a very compact package. Although the first Cambridge pocket computer was already on the market, we were afraid it might be difficult to modify.

Thinking it would be easier to deal with, we bought an Ampro single-board computer. It was nothing more than a very small motherboard (about six by eight inches) using a V40 CPU, with built-in video and disk controllers. To provide the voice output and menu capability, we used a Heathkit HV-2000 speech synthesizer, which was on a small circuit board about four by five inches in size.

Although the Ampro board was a CMOS design, it drew almost one ampere of current from a five-volt power supply. Added to the power required by the radio transmitter, we went through batteries too fast. We ultimately replaced it with a Zeos pocket computer, which turned out to be more satisfactory. The Zeos was less than an inch thick and was powered by two AA cells that lasted all night.

Preparing the Computer

Based on our experience, the easiest approach to the hardware problem is to use a commercial pocket computer. Although Zeos no longer offers one, there are many other brands to choose from, such as Casio, Hewlett-Packard, NEC, Philips, Psion, and Sharp.

When selecting a particular model, check that the internal memory isn't taken up with nondeletable built-in programs such as word processors, scheduling calendars, and phone directories. Any shell program such as Windows is detrimental and should be removed. Even if you are an old-time minimalist programmer, you will probably need at least 300 KB (kilobytes) of available RAM. The computer should be DOS-compatible and include a transfer cable and software so that external files can be loaded from your PC. If you can get one of those "personal organizers" to work, that would be a very inexpensive way to go.

Ultimately, the pocket computer will have to be brought into a casino, hidden under a person's clothing. By necessity, the case will be closed, eliminating direct access to the keyboard. Therefore, after obtaining the computer, you will have to get inside to connect wires for the external timing switches and to bring out wires from the speaker output. Some pocket computer cases are tricky to get open and trickier to put back together, so getting some service information would be helpful. When someone tells you that opening the computer case will void the warranty, invent your own smart-ass retort.

The technician entering the case should take the necessary precautions to avoid static electricity damage. That person should also have a set of miniature tools handy, including tweezers and a small grounded soldering iron with a needle tip. If the person doing this is not experienced in working with CMOS circuitry, the computer will almost certainly be destroyed by static electricity.

In our project, three push-button switches provided sufficient flexibility to operate all the menu and timing functions. On the Zeos, the external buttons were connected to the keyboard letters m, j, and u. These had the most accessible keyboard circuit-board traces with the roomiest soldering pads. Pocket computers are so tight and compact inside that the thickest wire you can use will be about 28 or 30 gauge. This size of wire is too fragile for use on the outside, so a transition to heavier wires needs to be made where they exit the case.

A miniature connector would be a good solution for the wire transition, but you will need some ingenuity in finding a place to mount it. If three buttons are used, one wire for each letter plus a common wire will be needed, and two more wires for the speaker line. This will require at least a six-pin connector. In addition, to save battery power, you may want to add another pair of wires for an external on/off switch.

The external cable should be made long enough to reach from wherever the computer is positioned to wherever the switches are located. Typically, this would be from one armpit (the computer) to a side pants pocket (the switches). A miniature snap-action normally-open push-button switch such as the Cutler-Hammer series PS or the Alcoswitch series MPS works well for the main timing button. If the same type of switch is used for all three push-buttons, try each of them first and select the one with the best touch to be the main timer button. Mount the switches in a small container that feels comfortable when the thumb is over the switch button.

Although the modified pocket computer could be used for testing, because of the larger screen and keyboard, we found it easier to use an old Toshiba laptop for both testing and refining the characterization data out in the field. To modify the laptop for testing, a 3.5mm miniature phone socket was installed in the case and internally connected to a letter on the keyboard. In this way, an external timer button or the output from an optical sensor (see below) can be plugged in, as needed. If a desktop PC is being used for testing, install the miniature phone socket in its keyboard.

Selecting the Radio Gear

A large assortment of portable two-way radio equipment is available in the marketplace. You can find a pair of miniature, low-powered walkie-talkies that would do the job just fine in almost any consumer-electronics superstore. The needed modifications are quite simple. Start by disconnecting the microphones and speakers of both walkie-talkies. On the unit that will be used by the timing person, connect the speaker output wires from the computer through a resistive attenuator to the microphone input-line of the walkie-talkie. For the bettor's unit, simply connect a suitable earphone to the speaker output line. That is all there is to it.

Although it has some disadvantages, there is a very good reason for using an FM transmitter instead of walkie-talkies: The only gear that has to be carried by the bettor is an ordinary unmodified FM broadcast-band radio, such as a Walkman. In the unlikely event that the bettor is taken to a back room and subjected to a body search, the presence of a Walkman would not be incriminating, but finding a modified walkie-talkie would raise serious suspicions.

One disadvantage of the FM transmitter is that it is more likely to be overheard by someone else carrying a Walkman or other broadcast-band FM radio. To protect against this, the voice menu should use coded terms that are not suggestive of roulette, or any gambling game for that matter. The other disadvantage is that the FM receiver has to be preset to the correct spot on the broadcast band, and could inadvertently be mistuned.

If you decide to use an FM broadcast-band transmitter, avoid those cheap FM oscillators sold as wireless microphones; they are unstable and the frequency drift will be a real annoyance. A much better alternative is a crystal-controlled unit that uses an integrated circuit such as the Motorola MC2833P or the Rohm BA1404 stereo broadcaster. A complete FM transmitter kit using the BA1404 on a three-by-three inch circuit board, is available from DC Electronics, POB 3203, Scottsdale AZ 85271.

Acquiring A Roulette Wheel

Your program cannot be tested and debugged effectively without full access to a regulation roulette wheel. If you do not know someone who owns a wheel (and is willing to let you experiment with it), you will need to buy or rent one. The best way is to look in the Yellow Pages under Gaming Equipment & Supplies. Even in places where casino gambling is not legal, there will be merchants that provide gaming equipment for parties and charity casino nights. Many of these businesses can obtain regulation roulette wheels, and in most states there are no laws controlling the sale of gambling equipment.

Not surprisingly, the best selection and lowest prices of new and used wheels will be found in the State of Nevada. However, buying a roulette wheel in Nevada is not easy. Casino-quality wheels can only be sold by licensed suppliers. There is a five-day waiting period during which the Gaming Commission reviews the buyer's application and does a background check. Nevada residents who are not felons get routinely approved, but all the suppliers to whom I spoke said they have never seen an out-of-state buyer get an approval.

Of course, there are always ways to beat the system. One way is to buy an undersized wheel. A wheel that is less than 32 inches in diameter is not considered to be a gaming device by the Nevada Gaming Commission. The only problem is that most "homestyle" wheels are cheaply made. If you decide to get a small wheel, try the Gambler's General Store on South Main Street in Las Vegas. They carry a high quality 30-inch wheel that may be suitable for testing.

If you are really serious about the project, however, you should go to the trouble and expense of obtaining a full-size casino-quality wheel. In Nevada it will take some legwork: check with the smaller gaming suppliers, check the classifieds in the local papers, and generally ask around. Although buying a wheel in most other states will be simpler, you will probably pay more and may have to buy out of a catalog, which is not a good idea because you cannot verify the quality.

A 32-inch regulation wheel can be easily transported in a station wagon or a hatch-back sedan and will fit into the trunk of most full-sized cars and many compacts. Since a crated roulette wheel can weigh one hundred pounds or more, one person should not try to load it without help. When transporting an uncrated wheel, use plenty of padding and block the wheelhead so it is not resting on its bearings. Keep in mind that it is against Federal law to move gaming equipment across a state line without a permit. Although this law is not rigorously enforced (how can it be?), if you have to move a roulette wheel from state to state, be discreet.

Before buying a roulette wheel, examine it thoroughly. Whatever you do, avoid buying a wheel sight unseen, especially if the price seems like a bargain. Unless the seller is naive, a good quality full-size wheel will cost at least five or six thousand dollars, whether new or used. Most older wheels take on antique value, which keeps the price from falling. Before opening your wallet, be sure to check the following items:

1. Run your fingers along the ball track. It should feel reasonably smooth with no apparent bumps or irregularities.

2. Spin a ball on the track. It should roll with reasonable smoothness and with a minimum of rattle and bounce. Do this in both directions. Don't expect a velvety-smooth track unless you are paying more than ten thousand for the wheel.

3. Spin the ball several times and watch the drop point. Be sure the ball doesn't always drop from the same point on the track perimeter.

4. Rotate the wheelhead until it is turning at about one revolution every two seconds. If it has a decent bearing, it should rotate on its own for at least three minutes before coming to a complete stop. Do this test in both directions.

5. While the wheelhead is rotating, look for any wobble or rise and fall in its motion by observing the outer edge of the wheelhead at several points around the perimeter of the bowl. Be sure the gap where the edge of the apron meets the edge of the wheelhead remains constant.

6. Check that the outer edge of the wheelhead and the edge of the apron are exactly even. If one edge is higher than the other, be sure the wheel has a height adjustment and that the problem can be corrected. Note that most cheaper wheels do not have a height adjustment for the wheelhead, which is OK if the two edges are reasonably even to begin with.

Building an Optical Sensor

An automatic timing device is almost a necessity for testing the program on a roulette wheel. When the testing and debugging sessions extend into the night, concentrating on the reference mark and clicking the timing button gets very tiring. Prediction inaccuracies will then be blamed on timing errors, which may or may not be the reason. Without some kind of automatic timing aid, there is simply no way of being certain.

An optical sensor that can "see" the ball every time it passes the reference mark will eliminate any doubt as to timing accuracy during testing and will reduce the overall fatigue level. Since such a device is not available commercially, you will need to design and build your own. To save design time, a suggested schematic for a simple optical pulse detector is provided in Figure 16-1.

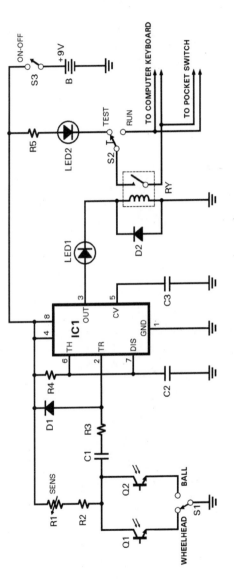

Figure 16-1 Electrical Diagram for Optical Plus Detector

PARTS LIST FOR OPTICAL PULSE DETECTOR

SEMICONDUCTORS
D1, D2 — 1N4148 diode
IC1 — NE555 timer
LED1 — light-emitting diode, green
LED2 — light-emitting diode, red
Q1, Q2 — 4N33 NPN phototransistor

RESISTORS
R1 — 10,000 ohm trimpot
R2, R4 — 1000 ohms, 1/4 watt
R3 — 10,000 ohms, 1/4 watt
R5 — 220 ohms, 1/4 watt

CAPACITORS
C1 — 0.001 : F ceramic
C2 — 0.1 : F mylar
C3 — 0.01 : F ceramic

OTHER PARTS
B — 9 volt battery
RY — SPST, N.O. relay, reed,
    coil: 5vdc, 200-400 ohms
S1 — SPDT miniature toggle switch
S2 — SPDT push-button switch
S3 — SPST miniature toggle switch

The pulse detector input consists of two phototransistors, one for sensing the ball and the other for sensing the wheelhead rotation. Both phototransistors are electrically connected as diodes with the base connection open-circuited. Manual switches on the control-box determine which of the two phototransistors is active, so that the optical pulses can originate either from the passing ball or from a passing white marker on the rotating wheelhead.

The optical signal triggers an NE555 timer that, operating in its monostable mode, drives a reed relay. The relay contacts, which simulate a manual timing button, are connected to the test computer.

The emitter and collector leads of each phototransistor are soldered to a twisted pair of 18-gauge solid copper wires, which can be easily repositioned by bending. The phototransistors and their connections are covered with short pieces of shrink tubing. The two twisted pairs go to a connection box mounted on the rim of the roulette wheel with double-backed tape. A three-conductor cable carries the optical signals back to the control box, which contains the battery, the switches, and the rest of the circuitry.

A bright light should be focussed at the section of the wheel where the two phototransistors are aimed. The white ball is an ideal optical trigger, and a narrow strip of white tape acts as an optical marker for the wheelhead. To provide adequate light contrast, some black tape may also be needed to improve the background separation.

Speech Synthesis

As mentioned earlier, our first attempt at using a voice output and a voice menu, was by means of the Heathkit HV-2000 speech synthesizer (which is no longer available). With the Zeos computer, we switched to a pure software solution to eliminate the extra circuit board. A number of shareware programs are available for generating synthesized speech without any added electronics. Some of the shareware providers also offer a service of making custom voice files, or you can make your own. With the sound boards and MIDI setups available today, this is relatively easy to do.

WINNING THE MONEY

Because of the economic power wielded by the gambling industry, the laws in the states of Nevada and New Jersey make it very
tough on anyone who is caught cheating a casino. To make it even
tougher on the player, the term *cheating* (and its various synonyms)
is very ambiguous, in that it is defined differently in different
places and at different times. For instance, in the State of Nevada, mentally keeping track of exposed cards to gain an advantage while playing blackjack is considered cheating. If the casino
even *suspects* that a player is counting exposed cards, they have
the legal right to evict that person from the premises.

In New Jersey, mentally counting cards at blackjack was, by court
decree, considered a legitimate technique for playing the game.
That is, until the Atlantic City casinos spent hundreds of thousands of dollars in legal fees to get the New Jersey Supreme Court
to rule otherwise. Interestingly, the Court did not include games
such as bridge, pinochle, hearts, or gin rummy in its card-count-
ing ban.

Although the term *cheating* has a moralistic ring to it, in gambling casinos, it is strictly a legal issue. Anytime a player devises a
playing technique that reduces the house profit on a game, the
casino tries to categorize the new method as a form of cheating
and usually manages to get local laws enacted against its use. This
was the case with calculators and computers. The casinos never
worried much about such devices until they learned that some
ingenious players were using computers to help them gain an
advantage. It was not long before the laws were enacted.

The problem with this is that the gambling business operates
under a double standard, and the local authorities who benefit
financially from the presence of the casinos, enforce that double

standard. Some casinos have set up games in which the house percentage is unconscionably high—tantamount to stealing, but perfectly legal. In most places, casinos have the legal right to force a consistently-lucky winner to leave the premises, whereas an unlucky loser can remain until he runs out of money and assets. In fact, American casinos do not hesitate to drain a compulsive gambler until he is bankrupt. It appears that in the gambling business, the concept of "morality," if it exists at all, is very one-sided.

Apart from cheating, the entire issue of gambling is a moral taboo for many people and a moral dilemma for others. The same appears to be true for the various state governments in the United States. Although most states legally prohibit gambling on moral grounds, many of these same states encourage their residents to buy lottery tickets. Furthermore, the odds of winning most state lotteries are so poor and the payoffs are so paltry that they make the casinos look like philanthropists.

The point to this discussion is that there is no moral issue connected with any method a clever person can devise to beat a casino game; the only issues are legal ones. And, as we have mentioned, the laws are arbitrarily designed to protect casino profits and to make sure that the "games of chance" really are not that chancy for the casino. Historically, gambling casinos have cheated players thousands of times more often than players have managed to cheat the casinos. Since cheating was originally and extensively practiced by the gambling halls and casinos, that makes them fair game.

In fact, under some circumstances, the issue of gambling itself may not even exist. If you devise a method for consistently beating a game, you have eliminated the element of chance and playing that game is, by definition, no longer a gamble.

Casino Surveillance
Whenever people handle large flows of money, it seems to be a natural law that the minds of many of them should work overtime at devising ways to divert the flow. It is not surprising, there-

fore, that the preponderance of cheating and outright theft in casinos is done by their own people. Consequently, casino surveillance systems are primarily set up to observe and monitor the actions of dealers and other employees.

In earlier days, casino surveillance was often accomplished by a spotter sitting in an elevated chair overlooking the pit area. Evidence of this can still be found in some older casinos, especially in the baccarat areas. If you happen to be in Laughlin, Nevada, look in the old Regency Casino, which has a high chair at one end of the blackjack pit. While there, stay for dinner—the restaurant at the Regency is the best food bargain in town.

As newer casinos were built, they also got larger, and many of them went to a system of catwalks that were installed above a false ceiling with observation windows. By using tinted glass or one-way mirrors and keeping the light level low in the catwalk area, the surveillance personnel were not visible from the casino floor. This worked okay for overall observations, but to get a close look at any table, the use of binoculars was necessary.

Today, almost all casinos use closed-circuit television cameras. In the most sophisticated installations, many cameras can be remotely aimed in any direction and can be zoomed in to get a tight view of the table action. The surveillance room, with its bank of monitors, is just a phone call away from any of the pits. A call from a suspicious pit boss can initiate a closeup view of any table and record the results on a video tape.

Even in large casinos, there are rarely more than two or three observers watching the monitors in the surveillance room. Besides the gaming tables, surveillance cameras can be found in the keno area, the poker room, the money counting room, the cashier's cage, and throughout the slot machine areas. Obviously, monitoring all the playing tables all the time is not possible. In fact, until a phone call comes in from a pit boss, the surveillance personnel are more likely zooming in on cleavages.

A misconception harbored by some people is that the video surveillance cameras can photograph and clearly identify individual players. This is not very likely, since the cameras are above the playing areas and only get a good view of the tops of peoples heads or, at best, a view from an oblique downward angle. Of course, you can always cooperate by tilting your head back and smiling at the camera. To be sure they cannot get a good look at your face, just wear a baseball cap with the bill pointed forward.

It is true that if casino personnel decide that your presence is not desirable, they try to get a photo of you for their records. This is easily accomplished by a security employee with an ordinary film camera, and if you did not notice the flash, you wouldn't even realize that they took your picture. They will then add your photo to their rogues' gallery, which is usually near the dealer's locker room, in a spot where the casino employees always pass.

Pit Psychology

Before launching a project that a casino might find objectionable, it would be time well spent to study pit activities and the behavior of pit personnel. Knowing the difference between routine behavior and non-routine behavior is essential. When one is engaged in any kind of nefarious undertaking, the pit should be continually monitored for any unusual activity. It is always better to cash in and walk away before any concerns of the pit personnel escalate too far.

Most of the time, the floor supervisors casually wander around the pit area looking indifferent. The first clue that suggests something out of the ordinary may be happening is when they stop looking so bored. Typically, they will start whispering to each other while furtively glancing at a particular table. These people are not masters of subtlety, so once you are aware of what to look for, you will find their actions to be almost comically obvious.

Floor supervisors never act as individuals. Anyone that has a suspicion about something always gets someone else in the pit to verify that suspicion before any further action is taken. Everything is done on a consensus basis. If they all agree that something fishy is going on, then the next step they take is to start making phone calls.

The first call is probably to the surveillance room telling the operator to zoom in on the suspicious table and to start recording a video tape. A second call would show that they are really worried, since it is probably to the shift manager. By now, you should have cashed in and left the table, because the next phone call would be to security, asking them to send someone over to snap your picture.

It is also good to be aware of the hierarchy of suspicious characters. Whenever the pit supervision perceives something dubious at a particular table, the number-one suspect is the dealer, followed closely by any unaccompanied males at the table. In rare situations, if they had no other suspects, they might speculate about a male/female couple. Unaccompanied women, however, are never considered smart enough or nervy enough to put something over on the casino. This attitude about women, by the way, is also held by many female pit supervisors.

Whenever working a new casino, pay attention to when shift changes occur. Depending on the casino and the particular pit, swing shift can start as early as four p.m. or as late as eight p.m. If possible, avoid working through a shift change. A good procedure is to take a break that lasts from at least thirty minutes before the change to at least thirty minutes after the change. If you are winning steadily, or there is the slightest suspicion of some irregularity, the outgoing pit boss may point you out to the incoming pit boss. However, if you are not there at the time, you cannot be singled out.

Team Selection And Behavior

If more than one person is available to do the timer function in a computer prediction team, the obvious step is to set up a reaction-time test. This is a good approach, but be aware that the actual reaction time is less important than timing consistency. If all of the timing clicks are off by the same amount, there will no detrimental effect on the prediction.

The bettor can be anyone who understands the numbers in the earphone and can quickly lay down the right bets. A more professional bettor is one who can memorize the wheelhead number sequence so well that when the computer throws out a single number, the bettor can instantly lay down a ten- or twelve-number spread. The advantage to this is speed and simplicity. With the added betting speed, the timing person can click on the ball at the third or fourth turn prior to the drop point rather than the fourth or fifth turn, resulting in a significant accuracy improvement.

While engaging in a project, the best way to avoid pit scrutiny is for everyone to blend in and look as normal as possible. Unless you are at an exotic location, such as Casino de Monte Carlo, dress down rather than dress up. If you dress like a high roller, you will be noticed; if you dress like a middle-class slob, you will be ignored—until you start winning big.

For obvious reasons, changing your normal everyday appearance while you are working the wheel, is a good idea. If your hair is dark, wear a blond wig and vice-versa. If you normally do not wear eyeglasses, get a pair with weak or nonmagnifying lenses. If you wear rimless glasses, get a pair of heavy hornrims and vice-versa. All this applies to both males and females. Most men will need to wear a wig, if only to cover the earphone. With so many people carrying Walkmen, an earphone may seem innocuous, but any action that attracts the slightest bit of attention from the pit is not good procedure.

As we pointed out earlier, couples and unaccompanied women are generally paid little attention. This is a major clue in how to set up a team. In a computer prediction team, the timing person carries all the incriminating hardware and should, therefore, preferably be a woman. To provide a place for the timing button, she needs to be wearing loose slacks with side pockets. She should wear conservative clothes and little makeup to assure being ignored by the male pit employees.

If the timing person has to be a man, being accompanied by a woman seated in the chair nearest the wheel, has some advantages. He can then stand between her and the wheel, which gets him very close to the wheel without it appearing unnatural. Should the woman be well endowed and wearing a low-cut blouse, she will also serve as a distraction to male dealers and floor supervisors. This can be helpful in diverting attention from the bettor at the other end of the table, who is often laying down late bets. The only down-side to this arrangement is that it may take awhile to get the woman seated in the correct position. In this respect, if the man is alone, he will have more flexibility of movement, but may also be subject to more scrutiny.

Always be wary of female dealers and pit personnel, as not much can be done to divert their attention for more than a moment or two. Any female player at the table purposely distracting the male dealers, will be looked on with some suspicion by many female supervisors. Therefore, this type of distraction should be done in a guileless, innocent-appearing manner.

Except those behaving as a couple, team members should enter and leave the casino separately and always act as strangers. When everything is working right and the chips are piling up in front of the bettor, avoid attracting attention by not running up more than $20,000 before cashing in. When working a small casino, hold it down to $5,000. After converting the roulette chips, leave the casino property immediately without stopping at the cashier's cage. Then have other team members come back in and cash the value chips in amounts of $1000 or less, so the cashier does not even *think* about filling out an IRS 1099 form.

If the game was aborted in the middle of a profitable session, wait thirty to sixty minutes after the next shift change to start over. To the new pit crew, you will be strangers or "fresh blood".

Finding the Right Wheel

Finding the right wheel should not be a major problem, since more than 600 roulette wheels are currently in service in legal casinos in the United States, and there are more than 3000 worldwide. It is just a matter of persistence. Which particular wheels are the right ones depends on the nature of the project.

Systems players need a single-zero wheel and not much else. A friendly atmosphere and a few other players at the table would be pleasant. If you need a lot of time to make your calculations and betting decisions, try to find a seat at a crowded table where the game will run a little slower.

Biased wheel players need not be particular so long as the wheel has a playable bias. However, they should be working an area with an abundance of wheels to clock. The obvious examples would be Las Vegas (over 200 wheels), Reno/Tahoe (about 100), and Atlantic City (over 150). Outside the United States, tight concentrations of wheels are harder to find. One of the best places is London, with more than 100 single-zero wheels. If you are at all interested in South America, Mar del Plata in Argentina also has well over 100 single-zero wheels. In most countries, however, only a few wheels are found in any one geographic location.

The requirements for computer prediction players and visual trackers are very similar. Both prefer an older-style wheel with deep pockets (high frets) and a ball track with a distinct lip. This type of wheel usually exhibits less ball bounce or at least a predictable bounce. With the older-style ball track, the ball slows more before it falls off the track and drops directly into the wheelhead rather than spiraling down. These characteristics can easily be determined visually within a few minutes of observation.

A steady, moderately-slow-turning wheelhead is an advantage to the tracker, but not as important for computer prediction work. Wheelhead speed varies from dealer to dealer, but is also related to casino training, so that in some casinos the wheels, in general, rotate slower than in others.

For any computer prediction project, the nature of the pit should also be considered. Not all pits are alike; they tend to reflect the personality of the pit boss. As a result, some pits are more paranoid than others. Try to stick with pits that appear more relaxed and laid back, but remember that a new shift will also bring a new pit boss.

In Conclusion . . .

Thirty-five years ago, Dr. Edward Thorp published a book called *Beat the Dealer* that introduced the concept of mentally counting cards in the game of blackjack. Because Dr. Thorp convinced his readers that, by applying his methods, they could consistently win, blackjack became the most popular table game in casinos around the world. However, relatively few players applied Thorp's card counting methods with adequate skill, and the casinos earned more revenue on blackjack than ever before.

This book is expected to produce a similar result for roulette. If it is widely read, it will increase the popularity of roulette because players will no longer consider it an unbeatable game. However, most roulette players will not apply the techniques described in this book methodically enough or with sufficient skill to overcome the house advantage. As a result, the casinos will earn more money than ever which, hopefully, will encourage them to install more roulette wheels.

Today, slot machines are the most popular gambling devices in U.S. casinos and most Americans who take a holiday at a gambling resort allow the slots to grind away at their bankroll until it is all gone. If you used to play the slots almost exclusively and are now playing roulette, at least occasionally, this book has achieved its goal. If you used to play roulette with no logical plan for overcoming the house edge, and now you are successfully applying one or more of the techniques described in this book, we are pleased that we could help. You can return the favor by recommending this book to your friends.

APPENDIX
Where Are The Wheels?

The following is a run-down of where different types of roulette wheels are used in the world. Because casinos often make changes and new casinos open on a regular basis, the information presented below can only be considered a best effort as of this book's publication date.

Definitions of the three basic wheel types may be found in Chapter 1 and in the Glossary. To recap, the American roulette wheel has 38 numbers with a single zero and a double zero, while both the French and hybrid wheels have 37 numbers with just a single zero.

NORTH AMERICA
Bahama Islands
The American wheel is predominant throughout the Bahamas, with the following exceptions:

Paradise Island — Paradise Island Casino
San Salvador Island — Club Med Columbus Isle & Casino

Paradise Island has a French wheel and Club Med has a hybrid wheel.

CANADA
The American wheel is predominant throughout Canada, with the following exceptions:

Windsor, Ontario — Casino Windsor
Montreal, Quebec — Casino du Montreal
La Malbaie/Point-au-Pic, Quebec — Casino de Charlevoix

The previous casinos have hybrid wheels even though you would expect to find French wheels in Quebec.

CARIBBEAN ISLANDS
The American wheel is prevalent in the Caribbean Islands, except that a few French wheels can be found in the Dominican Republic, Martinique, St. Maarten, and Guadeloupe.

CENTRAL AMERICA
The American wheel is prevalent in Honduras and Panama, which are the only Central American countries where roulette is played.

UNITED STATES
With few exceptions, the American wheel is predominant. At the time this book was published, one or more single-zero hybrid wheels could be found at each of the following casinos:

Atlantic City, New Jersey — Merv Griffin's Resorts Casino
Atlantic City, New Jersey — Showboat Casino
Atlantic City, New Jersey — Trump Taj Mahal Casino
Atlantic City, New Jersey — TropWorld Casino
Atlantic City, New Jersey — Trump's Castle Casino
Atlantic City, New Jersey — Trump Plaza Casino
Ely, Nevada — Hotel Nevada & Gambling Hall
Henderson, Nevada — Eldorado Casino
Las Vegas, Nevada — Excalibur Casino
Las Vegas, Nevada — MGM Grand Casino
Las Vegas, Nevada — Monte Carlo Casino (10 wheels)
Las Vegas, Nevada — Riviera Casino
Las Vegas, Nevada — Sam's Town Gambling Hall
Las Vegas, Nevada — Stratosphere Casino
Reno, Nevada — Club Cal-Neva Casino
Stateline, Nevada (Lake Tahoe) — Caesars Tahoe Resort

SOUTH AMERICA

With the exception of Brazil and Guyana, casino gambling is generally legal throughout South America. In most countries the predominant casino language is Spanish. The casino business in many countries is unstable and frequent changes occur at the whims of the government.

Argentina
Number of casinos: 23
Types of wheels: All hybrid.
Note: The Central Casino in Mar del Plata is the largest in South America with well over 100 single-zero wheels.

Chile
Number of casinos: 6
Types of wheels: Mostly French, some hybrid.

Columbia
Number of casinos: 16, mostly small.
Types of wheels: Some French, probably some hybrid.

Ecuador
Number of casinos: 17
Types of wheels: Probably hybrid.

Paraguay
Number of casinos: 7
Types of wheels: American, French, and hybrid.

Peru
Number of casinos: 9
Types of wheels: Probably hybrid.

Uruguay
Number of casinos: 17
Types of wheels: All French.

Venezuela
Number of casinos: 11
Types of wheels: Probably hybrid.

EUROPE

Most European countries have legal casino gambling. There was a time when the only type of roulette wheel to be found in Europe was the French wheel. Sadly, this is no longer true, since many casinos now cater to American tourists, many of whom do not know the difference between single- and double-zero wheels.

The major concentrations of casinos are found in the following countries:

Austria
Number of casinos: 12
Types of wheels: French and hybrid.

Belgium
Number of casinos: 8
Types of wheels: Mostly American, some French.

Czech Republic
Number of casinos: 44, mostly small.
Types of wheels: All hybrid.

Finland
Number of casinos: 14, many are small.
Types of wheels: Mostly low-stakes French

France
Number of casinos: 140, mostly small.
Types of wheels: French, hybrid, and boule.

Germany
Number of casinos: 38
Types of wheels: Mostly French.

Hungary
Number of casinos: 21
Types of wheels: Mostly hybrid, some French.

Italy
Number of casinos: 4
Types of wheels: Mostly French.

Monaco
Number of casinos: 4
Types of wheels: French at Casino de Monte Carlo; hybrid at the other three.

Netherlands
Number of casinos: 10
Types of wheels: Mostly hybrid, some French.

Poland
Number of casinos: 13
Types of wheels: Probably hybrid.

Portugal
Number of casinos: 8
Types of wheels: Mostly French, without en prison rule.

Romania
Number of casinos: 6
Types of wheels: Probably hybrid.

Russia
Number of casinos: 46, unstable.
Types of wheels: Probably hybrid.

Spain
Number of casinos: 25
Types of wheels: Mix of American, French, and hybrid.

Sweden
Number of casinos: 13, mostly small.
Types of wheels: Low-stakes French.

Turkey
Number of casinos: 70
Types of wheels: All hybrid.

Ukraine
Number of casinos: 16
Types of wheels: Mostly hybrid.

United Kingdom
Number of casinos: 130
Types of wheels: All hybrid.
Note: London has 20 casinos with a total of over 100 single-zero
wheels.

ASIA AND SOUTH PACIFIC

Australia
Number of casinos: 9
Types of wheels: Mostly American. Hybrid wheels can be found
in Canberra and Tasmania.

Macao
Number of casinos: 8
Types of wheels: Hybrid and boule. No en prison rule.

Nepal
Number of casinos: 4
Types of wheels: All hybrid.

Philippines
Number of casinos: 11
Types of wheels: All American.

South Korea
Number of casinos: 13
Types of wheels: Mostly American.

AFRICA AND INDIAN OCEAN

Many countries in Africa and the Indian Ocean Islands have one or two casinos, but information about them is sketchy. The major casinos are in the following countries:

Egypt
Number of casinos: 14
Types of wheels: Mostly American.

Kenya
Number of casinos: 9
Types of wheels: American and hybrid.

Mauritius Islands
Number of casinos: 9
Types of wheels: American and possibly some French.

Nigeria
Number of casinos: 8
Types of wheels: Probably American.

South Africa
Number of casinos: 9
Types of wheels: All hybrid.

ACKNOWLEDGEMENT

In addition to personal observation, much of the material in this appendix was obtained from: *Casinos – The International Casino Guide*, fifth edition, B.D.I.T., Port Washington, NY, 1996.

BIBLIOGRAPHY

ROULETTE BOOKS

Allen, J. Edward, *The Basics of Winning Roulette*. Cardoza Publishing, New York, 1993. One of the best little booklets on how to play roulette.

Barnhart, Russell T., *Beating the Wheel*. Carol Publishing, New York, 1994. The only book devoted entirely to clocking and playing biased roulette wheels.

Bass, Thomas A., *The Eudaemonic Pie*. Vintage Books, Random House, New York, 1986. An account of a group of scientists who designed and built a computer for beating roulette wheels.

Julian, John F., *The Julian Strategies in Roulette*. Paone Press, Lynbrook, NY, 1992. Some unique approaches to roulette betting systems and strategies.

Korfman, Tony, *Roulette – Playing to Win*. Gaming Books, Las Vegas, 1986. A simple guide to playing roulette, plus some tips.

Leigh, Norman, *Thirteen Against the Bank*. Oldcastle Books, London, 1991. The story of an Englishman whose team of roulette system players broke the bank at the Municipal Casino in Nice.

Nolan, Walter I., *The Facts of Roulette*. Gambler's Book Club, Las Vegas, 1978. A good little booklet on how to play roulette.

Patrick, John, *So You Wanna Be a Gambler – Advanced Roulette*. Gambler, Metuchen, NJ, 1987. An idiosyncratic book on money management and betting systems. Abridged version printed in 1996 by Carol Publishing under the title *John Patrick's Roulette*.

Shelley, Ron, *A Roulette Wheel Study*. Ron Shelley, Atlantic City, 1992. An unusual self-published manual on the construction and characteristics of roulette wheels by an expert in the business.

Squire, Norman, *How to Win at Roulette*. Oldcastle Books, London, 1992. A good book on classical roulette betting systems.

Taucer, Vic, *Roulette Dealing and Supervising*. Casino Creations, Las Vegas, 1994. One of the best instruction manuals for training roulette dealers and supervisors.

GLOSSARY

Advantange — See HOUSE ADVANTAGE.

American Number Sequence — The sequence of numbers found on the wheelhead of an American roulette wheel. Starting clockwise from zero, the numbers are: 0-28-9-26-30-11-7-20-32-17-5-22-34-15-3-24-36-13-1-00-27-10-25-29-12-8-19-31-18-6-21-33-16-4-23-35-14-2.

American Wheel — A roulette wheel containing 38 ball pockets, numbered 1 through 36, plus 0 and 00, using the American number sequence, and having a betting layout that uses English terminology. Also called a double-zero wheel.

Ball — A small ball which is spun around the ball track of a roulette wheel. The ball is usually white and has a diameter of about 13/16 inch.

Ball Deflector — An oblong deflector in the bowl below the ball track of a roulette wheel, designed to increase the random motion of the ball after it leaves the track and before it lands in a pocket. A typical wheel has either 8 or 16 deflectors. Also called canoe stop because most deflectors are shaped like tiny upside-down canoes.

Ball Track — The circular groove inside the rim of a roulette wheel bowl where the ball spins. Also called track or race.

Bank — (a) The money on the table that is used by the dealer to pay winning bets. (b) The casino or the game operator.

Biased Wheel — A roulette wheel that repeatedly favors a certain number or group of numbers, instead of being random.

Bimodal Bias — A type of wheel bias that favors two separated numbers or two contiguous groups of numbers.

Black Bet — An even-money bet on the 18 black numbers.

Blacks — Black casino checks with a value of $100 each.

Bleeder — A paranoid casino supervisor that worries about players winning. Also called a sweater.

Bowl — The outside part of a roulette wheel that houses the revolving wheelhead. The bowl contains the circular ball track. Also called rim.

Button— See LAMMER.

Buy-In — (a) An exchange of a players currency for casino chips or checks. (b) The amount of money a player gives the dealer for the chips or checks.

Cancellation System — See LABOUCHERE SYSTEM.

Canoe Stop — See BALL DEFLECTOR.

Carre — The French term for a corner bet.

Casino Advantage — See HOUSE ADVANTAGE.

Check or Cheque — Alternate term for CHIP that is commonly used by casino personnel and professional gamblers.

Checkracker — An additional dealer who assists the roulette dealer by picking up and stacking used checks. Also called a mucker.

Cheval — The French term for a split bet.

Chip— A gaming token with an imprinted value that is used in place of real money at various games in a casino. Chips may be redeemed for cash at the issuing casino. Also called house check, casino chip or value chip. Note: The terms CHIP and CHECK are often used interchangeably. See also ROULETTE CHIP.

Clocking— (a) The collecting and recording of winning numbers to see if a roulette wheel exhibits any bias. (b) Any study of a wheel to see if it has non-random characteristics.

Colonne — The French term for a column bet.

Column Bet — A bet on one of the three long columns on the roulette layout. Each column contains 12 numbers and pays 2 to 1.

Combination Bet — Any bet where a single check or a single stack of checks crosses a line and covers more than one number.

Contiguous Number Group — A group of numbers on a wheelhead that are directly adjacent to each other.

Corner Bet — A combination bet covering four numbers, that pays 8 to 1. Also called a square bet.

Croupier — The French term for a dealer.

Crown Marker — See WIN MARKER.

Cylinder — See WHEELHEAD.

D'Alembert System — An even-money betting system in which the bet is increased by one unit after every loss and decreased by one unit after every win. Also called a pyramid system.

Dealer — The casino employee that operates the roulette game.

Dealer Signature — The characteristic way a particular dealer spins the ball. This includes how fast the ball is launched, the type and amount of initial spin (english), and the dealer's consistency.

Double-Street Bet — See LINE BET.

Double Zero — One of the two green numbers on an American roulette wheel, the other green number being zero.

Double-Zero Wheel — See AMERICAN WHEEL.

Douzaine — The French term for a dozen bet.

Dozen Bet — A bet on the first, second or third dozen numbers on the roulette layout. These numbers are 1-12, 13-24 and 25-36, and each dozen pays 2 to 1.

Drop — The total money a roulette table takes in during one shift.

Drop Box — The locked cash box under the table into which the dealer inserts money received from the players.

Edge — A statistical advantage. Usually the casino's advantage.

English Wheel — Essentially an American wheel with the double zero eliminated. A result of the British Gaming Act of 1968. See HYBRID WHEEL.

En Plein — The French term for a straight-up bet.

En Prison — A rule applied in most European casinos to even-money outside bets when the winning number is zero. The player has the option of either losing half the bet or allowing the entire bet to be held over (imprisoned) for the next spin. See SURRENDER.

Even Bet — An even-money bet on the 18 even numbers. Zero and double zero are not considered even numbers.

Even Money — A bet that pays 1 to 1. Also called a flat bet.

Five-Number Bet — A combination bet covering the numbers 0, 00, 1, 2 and 3 that can only be made on an American wheel. It is known as a sucker bet because it pays only 6 to 1 and gives the house a 7.89 percent edge.

Flat Bet — A bet that pays 1 to 1. Also called even money.

Floorman — A politically-incorrect term for a floor person.

Floor Person — A floor supervisor.

Floor Supervisor — A pit supervisor who reports to the pit boss. This is the person who watches dealers to assure that all losing bets are collected, winning bets are correctly paid, and nobody is cheating.

French Number Sequence — The sequence of numbers found on the wheelhead of a French roulette wheel. Starting clockwise from zero, the numbers are: 0-32-15-19-4-21-2-25-17-34-6-27-13-36-11-30-8-23-10-5-24-16-33-1-20-14-31-9-22-18-29-7-28-12-35-3-26.

French Wheel — A roulette wheel containing 37 ball pockets, numbered 1 through 36, plus 0, using the French number sequence, and having a betting layout that uses French terminology.

Frets — The metal separators forming the numbered pockets in the wheelhead.

Gaff — A cheaters device or technique.

Gaffed Wheel — A rigged wheel that has been altered to favor the house.

Green Numbers — The zero and double zero.

Greens — Green casino checks with a value of $25 each. Also called quarters.

High Number Bet — An even-money bet on the 18 high numbers: 19-36.

House — The casino, the bank, or the game operator.

House Advantage — The difference between the actual odds on a wager and the payoff odds, usually stated as a percentage, which is the mathematical edge the house has over the player. Also called casino advantage, house edge, house percentage, P.C., or vigorish.

House Odds — The amount the house pays a winning bet, usually stated as an odds ratio such as 35 to 1. Also called odds paid or payoff odds.

House Numbers — The 0 and 00 numbers on the roulette wheel which do not pay off on outside bets.

Hybrid Wheel — Any roulette wheel with only a single zero and an English-language betting layout.

Impair — The French term for a bet on the odd numbers.

Inside Bet — A straight-up or combination bet placed directly on the numbers on the layout, including zero and double zero.

Juiced Wheel — A gaffed roulette wheel that is controlled by electromagnets.

Labouchere System — An even-money betting system in which the first and last numbers in a betting line are canceled after every win and the amount of the bet is added to the betting line after every loss. Also called a cancellation system.

Lammer — A small plastic disk with an imprinted number, used by the dealer to keep track of the value of a player's chips. Also called a button.

Layout — The green felt surface displaying the roulette numbers and betting options, on which the players place their bets.

Le Partage — Similar to the *en prison* rule, except that the player loses half of the bet and doesn't have the option of letting it ride. Applied in the United Kingdom. See SURRENDER.

Limit — See TABLE LIMIT.

Line Bet — A combination bet on the six numbers in two adjacent rows, that pays 5 to 1. Also called six-number bet or double-street bet.

Low Number Bet — An even-money bet on the 18 low numbers: 1-18.

Manque — The French term for a bet on the low numbers.

Marker— A credit slip or counter check payable to the casino and signed by a player. See also WIN MARKER.

Martingale System — An even-money betting system in which the bet is doubled after every loss and is reduced to the initial bet after every win. Also called a doubling system.

Maximum — See TABLE LIMIT.

Mechanic — A skilled dealer who uses sleight-of-hand to cheat.

Minimum — The smallest bet allowed at a table.

Mucker — See CHECKRACKER.

Neighbors Set — A straight-up bet on one number plus additional straight-up bets on the adjacent numbers on the wheelhead. The winning number pays 35 to 1.

Nickels — See REDS.

Noir — The French term for a bet on the black numbers.

Odd Bet — An even-money bet on the 18 odd numbers.

Odds — The ratio of the number of ways to win versus the number of ways to lose. For example, on a wheel with 38 numbers, the odds of correctly picking a single number are 1 to 37.

Odds Paid — See HOUSE ODDS.

Outside Bet — A bet on any of the betting options on the layout outside of the number field, that pay 1 to 1 or 2 to 1.

Pair — The French term for a bet on the even numbers.

Passe — The French term for a bet on the high numbers.

Past Posting — A late bet placed after the roulette ball has left the track and landed in a pocket.

Payoff Odds — See HOUSE ODDS.

P.C. — Gambler's abbreviation for percentage. See HOUSE ADVANTAGE.

Pit — The area behind the gaming tables that is restricted to casino employees.

Pit Boss — The supervisor who is responsible for the tables in a specific pit or gaming area. The pit boss reports to the shift manager.

Pocket — One of the numbered recesses in the wheelhead into which the ball may land.

Purples — Purple casino checks with a value of $500 each.

Pyramid System — See D'ALEMBERT SYSTEM.

Quarters — See GREENS.

Race — See BALL TRACK.

Red Bet — An even-money bet on the 18 red numbers.

Reds — Red casino checks with a value of $5 each. Also called nickels.

Rigged Wheel — A roulette wheel that has been modified to favor either the house or the player. See GAFFED WHEEL.

Rim — See BOWL.

Rouge — The French term for a bet on the red numbers.

Roulette Chip — A gaming token with no imprinted value, used at roulette tables to avoid bet confusion by assigning each player a different color. Roulette chips have no intrinsic value and must be cashed in at the table that issued them. Also called color check, wheel check, or nonvalue chip. Note: The terms CHECK and CHIP are often used interchangeably.

Row Bet — See STREET BET.

Separators — See FRETS.

Shill — A casino employee who gambles with house money to stimulate interest in a game. Also called a prop.

Signature — See DEALER SIGNATURE or WHEEL SIGNA-TURE.

Single-Number Bet — See STRAIGHT-UP BET.

Single-Zero Wheel — A French or hybrid roulette wheel. A 37-pocket roulette wheel that does not have a double zero.

Six-Number Bet — See LINE BET.

Split Bet — A combination bet covering two numbers, that pays 17 to 1.

Square Bet — See CORNER BET.

Straight-UP Bet — An inside bet on any single number, including zero and double zero, that pays 35 to 1. Also called single-number bet.

Street Bet— A combination bet on the three numbers in one row, that pays 11 to 1. Also called row bet.

Surrender — Identical to the *le partage* rule. For even-money outside bets, the player loses only half the bet when the winning number is zero or double zero. This rule is applied in Atlantic City on double-zero wheels only.

Sweater — See BLEEDER.

Table Limit — The largest bet allowed at a table, which may be increased for a high roller. Also called limit or maximum.

Toke — Short for token, a gratuity given to the dealer. To comply with IRS rulings, tips are placed into toke boxes and periodically divided between all the dealers, after taxes have been withheld.

Tourneur — The French term for the croupier who spins the ball.

Track — See BALL TRACK.

Tracker — See VISUAL TRACKER.

Value Chip — See CHIP.

Vigorish — See HOUSE ADVANTAGE.

Visual Tracker— A person that, by watching a spinning roulette ball and its relationship to the rotating wheelhead, tries to predict into what group of numbers the ball is likely to fall. Also called a tracker.

Voisins — The French term for an inside bet on a single number plus added bets on its neighbors to both sides of that number.

Wheelhead — The central rotating piece within the bowl of a roulette wheel that carries the numbers and the ball pockets. Also called cylinder.

Wheel Signature — The characteristics of a particular roulette wheel. This includes any bias traits, it's location in the casino, it's orientation on the table, and any physical distinctions (such as make, model, marks and scratches) that would help to identify it at a future time.

Win Marker — The object that a dealer places over the winning number on the layout to identify the winning checks. Also called crown marker.

Zero — (a) One of the two green numbers on an American roulette wheel, the other number being double zero. (b) The only green number on a French or hybrid roulette wheel.

Baccarat Master Card Counter
New Winning Strategy!

For the **first time**, Gambling Research Institute releases the **latest winning techniques** at baccarat. This **exciting** strategy, played by big money players in Monte Carlo and other exclusive locations, is based on principles that have made insiders and pros **hundreds of thousands of dollars** counting cards at blackjack - card counting!

NEW WINNING APPROACH

This brand **new** strategy now applies card counting to baccarat to give you a **new winning approach,** and is designed so that any player, with just a **little effort,** can successfully take on the casinos at their own game - and win!

SIMPLE TO USE, EASY TO MASTER

You learn how to count cards for baccarat without the mental effort needed for blackjack! No need to memorize numbers - keep the count on the scorepad. Easy-to-use, play the strategy while enjoying the game!

LEARN WHEN TO BET BANKER, WHEN TO BET PLAYER

No longer will you make bets on hunches and guesses - use the GRI Baccarat Master Card Counter to determine when to bet Player and when to bet Banker. You learn the basic counts (running and true), deck favorability, when to increase bets and much more in this **winning strategy**.

LEARN TO WIN IN JUST ONE SITTING

That's right! After **just one sitting** you'll be able to successfully learn this powerhouse strategy and use it to your advantage at the baccarat table. Be the best baccarat player at the table - the one playing the odds to **win**! Baccarat can be beaten. The Master Card Counter shows you how!

To order send just $50 (plus postage and handling) by check or money order to:
Cardoza Publishing, P.O. Box 1500, Cooper Station, New York, NY 10276

THE GRI ROULETTE MASTER
- Advanced Winning Roulette Strategy -

Here it is! **Finally**, Gambling Research Institute has released the **GRI Roulette Master** - a **powerful** strategy formerly used only by **professional** and high stakes players. This **strongman strategy** is **time-tested** in casinos and has proven **effective** in Monte Carlo, the Caribbean, London, Atlantic City, Nevada and other locations around the world. It's available here **now**!

EASY TO LEARN
The beauty of the GRI Roulette Master is that it's **easy to learn** and easy to play. Its simplicity allows you to **leisurely** make the **correct bets** at the table, while always knowing exactly the amount necessary to insure **maximum effectiveness**.

BUILT-IN DYNAMICS
Our betting strategies use the **built-in dynamics** of roulette and ensure that only the best bets are working for us. There are no hunches or second guessing the wheel - all you do is follow the instructions, play the necessary bets, and when luck comes your way, **rake in the winnings**.

BUILT-IN SAFEGUARDS
The GRI Roulette Master's **built-in safeguards** protect your bankroll against a few bad spins while allowing you to **win steady sums of money**. Not only does this strategy **eliminate the pitfalls** of other strategies which call for dangerous and frightening bets at times, but also, allows you three styles of betting: **Conservative** for players seeking a small but steady low risk gain: **Aggressive** for players wanting to risk more to gain more: and **Very Aggressive** for players ready to go all out for **big winnings**!

BONUS!!! - **Order now**, and you'll receive the **Roulette Master-Money Management Formula** ($15 value) **absolutely free**! Culled from strategies used by the top pros, this formula is an **absolute must** for the serious player. It's bound right into the strategy.

To order send just $25 (plus postage and handling) by check or money order to: Cardoza Publishing, P.O. Box 1500, Cooper Station, New York, NY 10276

WIN MONEY AT ROULETTE!
ORDER NOW!!!

Yes! I want to be a tougher roulette player and take advantage of this **powerful** **strategy**. Please **rush** me the **GRI Roulette Master** and bonus, Money Management Formula ($15 Value). Enclosed is a check or money order for $25 (plus postage and handling) made out to:

Cardoza Publishing, P.O. Box 1500, Cooper Station, New York, NY 10276

MC/Visa/Amex Orders Toll-Free in U.S. & Canada, 1-800-577-WINS

Include $5.00 postage/handling for U.S. orders; $10.00 for Can/Mex; HI/AK and other countries $15.00. Outside U.S., money order payable in U.S. dollars on U.S. bank only.

NAME _____ COMPUTER _____

ADDRESS_____

CITY _____ STATE _____ ZIP _____

MC/Visa/Amex Orders By Mail

MC/Visa/Amex # _____ Phone _____

Exp. Date _____ Signature _____

Order Today! Go for the Big Jackpot Win!

RO Secrets

INTERNET CASINO BETTING?
Yes - You Can Now Bet From Your Home!

The Era of the New Casino! - www.cardozacasino.com

Yes! It's happening now from internet casinos around the world. You can now can play all your favorite gambling games – blackjack, roulette, slots, keno, video poker, craps, and more – right from your home computer and go for the big winnings, just as if you were in the casino.

Real Play & Free Play

At some web sites you can play for free, but if you want to gamble for real from your home or office, internet gambling – the new casinos – has become a reality. Are you dealt a square deal? Is casino gambling on the internet legal? We'll talk about these isues and more.

Find Out More!

Our web site will keep you up to date and informed with the latest developments on this exciting new technology. Check out our site; there's no charge!

FREE GAMBLING INFORMATION
www.cardozapub.com

You'll also want to check out the new web site for Cardoza Publishing. Here, you'll find out the latest information on all our publications, receive the inside privy on the debut of our new **free gambling magazine**–right on the web–and be kept up to date on internet gambling, the latest gambling strategies, the tip of the week, hotel specials in Las Vegas, and other gambling meccas. It's all coming soon right at our web site, **www.cardozapub.com.**

We'll see you there!